朱昱

May 2005

Chicago, Illinois

INNOVATION—
THE MISSING DIMENSION

INNOVATION—
THE MISSING
DIMENSION

Richard K. Lester *&* Michael J. Piore

HARVARD UNIVERSITY PRESS

Cambridge, Massachusetts

London, England   2004

Library of Congress Cataloging-in-Publication Data

Lester, Richard K. (Richard Keith), 1954–

Innovation—the missing dimension / Richard K. Lester and Michael J. Piore.

   p. cm.

Includes bibliographical references and index.

ISBN 0-674-01581-9 (cloth : alk. paper)

1. Technological innovations—Economic aspects—United States.
2. New products—United States—Management.   I. Piore, Michael J.
II. Title.

HC110.T4L47 2004

658.5′14—dc22   2004052377

To Anne and to Rodney

PREFACE

The basic ideas that we develop in this book emerged primarily from a series of case studies of new product development in cellular telephones, medical devices, and garments, especially blue jeans. These studies, conducted from 1994 to 2002 as part of a research program at the MIT Industrial Performance Center, served both to suggest the ideas of the book and also to ground those ideas concretely. They were chosen to represent a range of different products and professional disciplines. The cell phone and medical devices cases are drawn from two of the most technologically dynamic sectors of the economy: the information/communications sector and the life sciences/health care sector. The third case is drawn from the apparel sector, where creativity tends to be associated more with fashion than with technological advance.

In each case we selected one company to study intensively, with repeated visits and multiple interviews. The material gathered in the core company was then supplemented by material gathered at other companies working on the same or similar products, either in collaboration with the first company or in competition with it. The supplementary interviews were less extensive and generally did not involve repeat visits. Each case includes companies from Western Europe and Japan as well as the United States. Initially, we had hoped that this geographic distribution would enable us to compare organization and practice across these three regions. But the material did not generate the kind of variation that would allow us to distinguish cultural, legal, or other country-level effects from those that resulted from differences in the companies or the products we were observing.

The case that came closest to our original design was cellular telephones. Here, we focused first on Motorola and the effort of its infrastructure division to design a new cellular base station platform. We then visited AT&T (now Lucent) in the United States, Ericsson and Nokia in Scandinavia, and Matsushita in Japan. All of these companies were designing and producing cellular infrastructure or had at one time done so. And they all were in the business of producing cellular telephone handsets.

In the garment industry, we focused on Levi Strauss and the design of blue jeans (Levi's), although we also interviewed design managers of Levi Strauss's Dockers division. The driver in jeans fashion at the time of our study was the effects produced in the finishing operations performed by laundries where the jeans are washed and abraded. We interviewed American Garment Finishers, a key jeans laundry in the United States working exclusively for Levis; Martelli, an independent laundry in Italy working for leading Italian producers of fashion jeans (Replay and Diesel); and Tornello, an Italian designer and producer of laundry equipment. We also interviewed Camaïeu, a very different apparel mass-marketing firm in France. In Japan we conducted interviews at Toray, a textile firm closely allied with a range of clothing manufacturers, and the apparel firm Onward Kashiyama.

In medical devices, the study centered on Aspect Medical Systems, at the time a small start-up firm developing a technology for measuring the effect of anesthesia upon the brain. We followed developments there during four separate visits over the course of a year and a half. We also conducted interviews at Hewlett Packard's

Medical Products Group (later spun off as part of Agilent Technologies) and at the biotechnology firm Chiron in the United States; at Daiichi Pure Chemicals, a Japanese company that had licensed technology from Chiron; at the medical systems division of Shimadzu Corporation, a diversified technology company based in Kyoto, Japan; and at Oticon, a Danish hearing-aid manufacturer known for its innovative management style and organizational structure.

In addition to these cases, our understanding has been greatly influenced by three other pieces of work. One of these is a doctoral dissertation on design and development in the automobile industry conducted at the Industrial Performance Center by Kamal Malek, who participated first as a research assistant and then as a collaborator in the early stages of our own work.

A second source of material and insight has been our continuing relationship with Lutron, a lighting controls company, and its founder, Joel Spira. This relationship, which long predates this study, has given us a longitudinal perspective on the issues involved in design and development that our case study interviews, conducted at a particular moment of time, could not provide. Spira and his colleagues have also served as a valuable sounding board for our ideas.

Third, to illustrate our argument we have drawn on a doctoral dissertation by Annabelle Gawer at MIT's Sloan School of Management on the relationship between Intel and the group of (mostly small) firms that design and develop the computer peripheral products on which Intel depends, and which in turn depend on Intel. Gawer's study focuses on how Intel thinks about and manages this process.

Finally, we have drawn upon the extensive literature on product design and development and also upon a series of interviews conducted at the very beginning of our research with colleagues at MIT who are themselves working on these problems or who are involved as practitioners in the design and development process.

CONTENTS

The test of a first-rate intelligence is the ability to hold two opposing ideas in mind at the same time and still retain the ability to function.   F. Scott Fitzgerald (1945)

INTRODUCTION

In the summer of 2003, Microsoft Corporation announced that it would no longer use grants of stock options to compensate its employees. Instead, the company would rely on actual awards of stock. For an internal corporate matter—and a fairly technical one at that—the Microsoft announcement attracted a remarkable amount of press coverage, with page 1 headlines in *The New York Times, The Wall Street Journal,* and a number of other publications. But as the commentary made clear, this was about much more than compensation or corporate book-keeping. Microsoft, the nation's largest and most successful technology company, had struck a chord that would resound throughout the U.S. economy.

The practice of granting stock options to employees had been a hallmark of the technology boom of the 1990s and had made many people very rich. But in the aftermath of the stock market crash of 2001, many of these unused options had become worthless. And the widespread practice of not deducting option compensation from reported company profits—a questionable accounting procedure that had mostly been ignored during the boom years—was now attracting growing criticism from investors. Microsoft's decision to eliminate the granting of options not only signaled its own transition from the explosive growth of the 1990s toward the more staid trajectory of a large, mature industrial corporation but also symbolized a broader retreat from the high-wire business practices of that frenetic decade. As a *Business Week* headline proclaimed, it was "the end of an era."

Such proclamations had appeared with some regularity since the close of the 1990s, as a succession of unwelcome events—the spectacular bankruptcies of high-flying firms, the slide into recession, the drying up of demand for information and telecommunications technology, massive layoffs in Silicon Valley and other centers of innovation, and a rash of business and financial scandals—each seemed to signify that the economic successes and excesses of that decade were finally over.

But as each nail was hammered into the coffin of the exuberant nineties, the debate about what the decade actually meant in economic terms only intensified. There was no denying that it had meant *something*. The period between 1992 and 2001 had encompassed the longest uninterrupted economic expansion in American history. At the beginning of the 1990s the U.S. economy was widely thought to be in serious and perhaps even irreversible decline. Many worried that America's industries were about to be overrun by leaner and more innovative foreign competitors. Yet by the end of the decade, with more than 20 million new jobs created, with both unemployment and inflation at historically low levels, with productivity growth approaching the halcyon rates of the 1960s, and with American firms leading the global race to exploit the most important new technologies, the U.S. economy was unquestionably the strongest in the world. Even the onset of recession in early 2001 did not seem to alter fundamentally the perception, both at home and abroad, of its underlying strength and competitiveness.

But when it comes to explaining that extraordinary economic renaissance, there has been much less agreement, and a lively debate about its causes continues today. The debate is important because the lessons that are extracted from that period will profoundly affect America's economic policies and its business practices during the coming decade. Two distinct views, opposite and contradictory, have dominated the discussion and continue to shape managerial practice and public policy. One of these emphasizes the expanding reach of market competition and the role of entrepreneurship in the American economy. It focuses on the ease with which Americans can go into and out of business, on the abundance of venture capital for start-ups and especially its role in fueling the expansion of new technology-based enterprises, on the mobility of the country's labor force, on the legal structure which makes it easy both to hire new workers and to release them when they are no longer needed, and on a highly competitive business environment that rewards success handsomely and punishes failure in a harsh but effective manner.

The second viewpoint focuses on the large corporate enterprise and on the radical changes in organizational structures and management practices that swept through these firms in response to the competitiveness crises of the 1970s and 1980s. This account contrasts the bloated, rigid, complacent conglomerates of that period with the leaner, more agile corporations of today. It especially emphasizes the importance of corporate focus and specialization—of clearly identifying the company's central mission and core competencies, shedding and reconsolidating poorly fitting functions, outsourcing production and other non-core activities, and modularizing production. It recognizes the critical role of new information technologies and efficient capital markets in aiding, abetting, and often driving all of this.

Both of these points of view are broad generalizations, of course, and it is not difficult to find exceptions. Even as many managers were embracing the notion of core competence during the 1990s, others were aggressively pursuing a contrary vision of business synergies. In the telecommunications industry, for example, the pursuit of synergies between print and electronic media, between content and distribution channel, and between different kinds of distribution channels led to a spate of mergers during the 1990s. The most admired corporation of the decade, General Electric, was in many ways an old-fashioned conglomerate. Nevertheless, each perspective—one emphasizing the expansion of market competition and the other stressing internal corporate transformations—remains very influential, and the wide gulf that separates them is of real importance, since these two explanations have quite different implications for how we might move to consolidate the economic gains of the 1990s.

No resolution of this debate is possible, however, without first considering another striking feature of the 1990s boom: the remarkable surge of innovation that took place during this period. Major fields of technology-based enterprise such as cellular telephone use, electronic commerce over the Internet, and biotechnology—all almost unknown at the beginning of the decade—had entered the economic mainstream by the time it was over. That the economy's revival and this technological cornucopia were connected has been widely assumed. But how? Was the surge of innovation mainly caused by the expanding reach of market competition—getting price signals right, using market-generated financial incentives to put more pressure on individuals and organizations to perform, providing additional encouragement for entrepreneurship? Or did it occur because companies learned to focus on their core competencies, to outsource non-core functions to others who could perform them more efficiently, and to adopt modular approaches to design and production? Or was the surge of innovation the result of a different set of factors altogether?

Of all the questions surrounding America's economic renaissance, these may be the most significant. If American businesses are to lay the groundwork today for a new period of growth, they need to draw the right lessons about the sources of innovation in our economy, since these capabilities, more than any other, will determine our future prosperity.

A central conclusion of this book is that neither of the prevailing accounts of America's economic successes during the 1990s can adequately explain our innovative performance during that period. We are in danger of learning the wrong lessons about innovation. As a result, we risk neglecting those capabilities that are the real wellsprings of creativity in the U.S. economy—the capacity to integrate across organizational, intellectual, and cultural boundaries, the capacity to experiment, and the habits of thought that allow us to make sense of radically ambiguous situations and move forward in the face of uncertainty.

To see what is missing from the current economic policy debate, it is necessary to understand what actually happens when firms innovate—in the laboratories, the design studios, the factories, and the executive offices of American businesses. This need for a bottom-up perspective on innovation was the starting point of our research. The centerpiece was a series of case studies of new product design and development. The central insight to emerge from these case studies is that the most important capability of the U.S. economy (and indeed of any advanced economy)—its ability to generate a stream of new products, to improve upon old ones, and to produce existing products in an increasingly efficient way— depends on two fundamental processes, which we call *analysis* and *interpretation*.

Analytical processes work best when alternative outcomes are well understood and can be clearly defined and distinguished from one another. Interpretive processes are more appropriate when the possible outcomes are unknown— when the task is to create those outcomes and determine what their properties actually are. These two ways of proceeding involve very different kinds of skills, different ways of working together, different forms of managerial control and authority, and, ultimately, different ways of thinking about the economy. And these differences are not merely ones of degree. The two processes are actually in fundamental opposition to each other, making it difficult for people to think about both of them at the same time. Yet the ability of businesses to think about these two approaches separately and to manage them simultaneously is the central challenge of product development. And finding a balance between them is the key to sustaining the innovativeness, and hence the competitiveness, of the U.S. economy as a whole.

Analysis is the easier process to understand and implement. It is essentially *rational decision-making*—an approach that underlies much economic and managerial theory as well as theories of scientific inquiry. It is also the standard approach to engineering that students are taught in engineering schools. What analysis comes down to, essentially, is problem solving. In this view, business consists of a series of discrete problems and an associated series of decisions and choices about which of those problems to solve and how best to solve them. In designing a new product, the product development manager first seeks to define a clear objective, usually based on research into customer needs, and then identifies the resources—human, financial, and technical—that are available to meet that goal, as well as the constraints on those resources. He then organizes a project to accomplish the goal. The key step is to divide the problem into a series of discrete and separable components and assign each one to a knowledgeable specialist. The solution is obtained by bringing the components together in some optimum combination as quickly and efficiently as possible.

In this way of looking at new product development, the manager plays two basic roles. In one, he is the lead problem-solver, the chief engineer. In the other, he is the negotiator or mediator who resolves conflicts among the goals of different organizational constituencies in order to create the clarity needed for efficient problem solving to proceed.

There are several difficulties with this view. One is that it presumes a clear and unambiguous notion of what the pieces of the product are and who the specialists are to whom they can be assigned. But when design practitioners talk about what they actually do, they often sound very uncomfortable with this characterization of the process. Joel Spira, the electrical engineer and designer who founded Lutron Corporation, a leading manufacturer of lighting controls, captured the nature of this discomfort. "By the time I see the parts clearly enough to divide the problem into independent pieces, I already have the answer . . . Without a solution, you cannot imagine what the parts are."

And without a problem, you cannot imagine what the solution is. But where do the problems come from in the first place? How do they come to be defined? The management literature emphasizes the importance of listening to the voice of the customer. But often the customer does not really know what she wants or needs. Indeed, the customer may have no perceived preexisting needs at all. What is the problem in this case? And how can you be sure that you are not solving the wrong one?

What we found from our case studies is that not all of the activity that takes place within firms, or in the economy more generally, is about solving problems. Our studies of new product development led us to conclude that an important component of innovation involves a different process, one that is not directed toward the solution of well-defined problems. Indeed, this process cannot be said to have a clear endpoint at all. Rather, it is ongoing in time. The activity out of which something innovative emerges—a new insight about the customer, a new idea for a product, a new approach to producing or delivering it—is what we call *interpretation*. The interpretive process has much in common with the ways that people within a linguistic community come to understand and communicate with one another and with others in different linguistic communities. In this interpretive way of looking at business, the role of the manager has less to do with solving problems or negotiating between contending interests than with initiating and guiding conversations among individuals and groups.

The analytical perspective dominates the scholarly literature on innovation, competitiveness, and economics, particularly in business and engineering schools. It is even more dominant in the practice of these occupations. By contrast, the interpretive view is not widely understood or even fully recognized. A basic objective of this book is to make interpretation more prominent and its implications clearer in the minds of today's managers.

However, the thrust of our argument is not to replace analytical with interpretive management. In economic organizations priorities must be set, decisions must be made, and particular products must be chosen and put into production. In this sense, the analytical dimension must take precedence over the interpretive. But the interpretive process determines the range of alternatives from which business choices are actually made. If the interpretive process is truncated or nonexistent, that range will be too narrow. Managers with strong analytical skills may choose the right alternative within that range, but they will be choosing the best of a bad lot. However well the choice of product is made, and however quickly and decisively it is put into production, it will be at a disadvantage in the marketplace because of this failure at the interpretive stage.

We believe that American businesses must strengthen the interpretive approach to a point where it can stand alongside analysis as a tool to cultivate innovation. To maintain their innovative capabilities, firms must continually seek out and participate in exploratory, interpretive conversations with a variety of interlocutors, and this will require a rebalancing of management strategies in the direction of interpretation.

A similar rebalancing is also necessary at the policy level. Today the spaces in our economy in which such interpretive conversations can take place are under pressure, as competitive forces arising from globalization, technological change, and deregulation build. These interpretive spaces do not grow up naturally in market economies. They must be created; and once created, they must be cultivated, renewed, and enriched. The current focus of economic policy is to extend the reach of the market. The goal is to strengthen the system of market signals and incentives required for clean, effective, and efficient analytical thinking and decision-making. But unless this analytical focus of policy is matched by greater attention to interpretive processes, there is a real danger that the innovative performance of the U.S. economy will falter.

Our argument is developed in stages. In Chapter 1 we introduce the three major case studies of product development and design—in cellular telephones, medical devices, and blue jeans—from which the main ideas in this book emerged. The chapter's central theme is the problem of how to integrate the efforts of large numbers of people, working in different technical fields and organizational units, into a practical, profitable product design. Organizational integration is one of the core managerial challenges of our time, and management experts have devised an arsenal of tools and strategies for dealing with it. In a very fundamental sense, the key innovations in each of the case studies grew out of an integration: in every case different domains of knowledge were brought together to form something new and original, and in the process the initial elements lost their identity and were no longer recognizable. But the managers and engineers in our case studies did not have a way of thinking or talking about integration in that sense. When they used the term, they generally meant the addition of departments or divisions to form a larger unit.

These two different understandings of integration reflect the more fundamental distinction between analysis and interpretation. In Chapter 2 we develop these concepts in more detail and show how the engineers and managers in our case studies were biased toward the analytical approach. But we also show that these people were actually engaged actively in interpretive processes, even though they had difficulty talking about them as such. We suggest that these interpretive activities were like open-ended conversations among people from different professional and organizational backgrounds.

In Chapter 3 we explore the manager's role in animating these conversations. We liken it to the role of the hostess at a cocktail party, identifying the "guests," bringing them to the party, suggesting who should talk to whom and what they might talk about, intervening as necessary to keep the conversations flowing, and generally navigating between the shoals of boredom and hostility, either of which would cause the party to break up and the participants to leave. We show that what emerges from these conversations, if they are sustained, is something very much like a language community. New products emerge out of that community.

In Chapter 4 we expand upon the cocktail party metaphor and show how the manager's role in interpretation is different in almost every respect from the more familiar analytical role. But the pull of the analytical approach is so powerful that most managers cannot conceive of an alternative. This problem is highlighted by examining two of today's most prominent prescriptions for managers: "Listen to the voice of the customer" and "Focus on your core competencies." We show how each of them could be understood interpretively but how managers in our case studies in fact gave both of them an analytical cast that obscured the importance of interpretation and undermined its role.

The conflict between analysis and interpretation is not merely the result of bias in the thinking and training of managers, however. There are deep contradictions between the two approaches that make it difficult to pursue them simultaneously within the same organization. In Chapter 5 we examine these conflicts in detail and show how, in spite of them, some of the firms in our case studies were able to combine the two approaches successfully. But these combinations were fragile, threatened not only by managers' unfamiliarity with interpretive processes but also by the intense pressures of economic competition. Ultimately, in a competitive business environment, analysis must prevail, or new products will never be defined in a way that allows them to be produced and brought to market. But competitive pressures also increase the difficulties of pursuing interpretation, and this creates the need for public spaces, insulated from competition, where interpretive conversation can be pursued more freely.

In the next two chapters we consider a range of possibilities, including sheltered spaces for interpretation carved out both within and among groups of firms. We focus mainly on two particular types of public space that proved important in our case studies: the regulatory arena (in Chapter 6) and the research university (in Chapter 7). We argue, though, that many of these spaces are threatened as a result of the adoption over the past decade of market-oriented reforms by business and government.

The final chapter draws together the strands of the argument and summarizes its implications. The emphasis is on how recognition of the interpretive dimension changes the way we think about the practice of engineering and management, about the economy, and, as a result, about the thrust of public policy. We suggest a number of specific actions to strengthen the interpretive capacity of the American economy. Above all, the interpretive perspective points to the importance of cultivating a tolerance for ambiguity—the critical resource from which true innovation derives—while preserving the system of market signals and the managerial skills required for efficient analytical decision-making.

INTEGRATION IN CELL PHONES, BLUE JEANS, AND MEDICAL DEVICES

1

In modern economies, the central organizational problem presented by new product development is integration. For some complex products like automobiles, thousands of people may be engaged in the process. But even for fairly simple new devices or modest improvements to existing products, scores or even hundreds of people participate in new product development—from numerous designers and manufacturing specialists to marketers, accountants, and financial experts. How can individuals with such a diversity of backgrounds and perspectives be joined in pursuit of a common goal? How can managers reach across organizational and even corporate boundaries to create profitable new products and services quickly and efficiently? How—to use a term coined by the former General Electric CEO Jack Welch—can product development organizations become boundaryless?[1]

The case studies we will describe in this book yield interesting and sometimes surprising answers to these questions.

The organizational issues we uncovered turned out to be a good deal more complicated than the term *integration* alone would suggest. While all the cases did indeed entail integration across existing boundaries—among the organization's own departments or divisions, between the company and its outside partners, and between the producer and the consumer—they also involved the creation of new boundaries and organizational frontiers. What the managers were doing, in fact, is better described as *boundary management* than as a movement toward a boundaryless corporation.

In recent years management theorists have devised a storehouse full of tools for managing across boundaries. These include flat, decentralized structures, network organizations, matrix management practices, multifunctional teams, team leadership skills, and a wide array of techniques for listening to the voice of the customer. But among the practicing managers with whom we spoke, these models and maxims often seemed to be mere placeholders. Lacking the content to be operable in the real world, they quickly degenerated into clichés. When prompted, the managers in our cases could usually spout the rhetoric of integration. But in the real world of new product development, most of them were much more comfortable talking about *policing* boundaries than about breaking them down.

Our initial round of company interviews was prompted by a desire to better understand this new movement toward integration and to assess its practical applications. We did not actually pre-select our cases along this dimension, although we certainly would have done so if we had been able to find out enough about them in advance. But whether by accident or design, integration turned out to be absolutely central in each of our case studies. Cellular telephones are the marriage of the radio and the telephone; fashion jeans bring together traditional workmen's clothing and laundry technology borrowed from hospitals and hotels; medical devices draw on both basic life sciences and clinical practice. Without integration across the borders separating these different fields, there would have been no new products at all.

Cellular Telephones

A cellular telephone system has four basic components: the handset, the base station, the base station controller, and the switch.[2] The telephone handset itself is essentially a radio. It transmits its signal to a base station (also in part a radio receiver and transmitter). Each base station has a limited geographical range; when the caller is in motion, calls are handed off from one base station to another. The separate base station territories are the cells from which the technology derives its name, and the hand-off from one cell to another distinguishes cellular from most other forms of radio and telephone communication.

The movement of calls between cells is managed by the base station controller. As the user approaches the boundary of the cell, the controller must first decide which of the adjacent cells the call should be handed off to and at what instant. An idle frequency in the newly selected cell is then assigned to the call, and the new frequency to which the call will be shifted is relayed to the caller's phone, via the original base station. All this must be executed without any interruption in service.

When a traveling (roaming) user turns on a phone to make or receive a call, the phone first registers its location with the nearest base station. This information is then forwarded to the local switching center, which in turn identifies the user's home location, verifies with the home switching center that the user is in good standing, and requests and receives the user's service profile, including information about her calling plan. When all this electronic bookkeeping is finished, a call can be made or received as if the user was in her home service area.

If the user is placing a call, it will be transmitted by radio to the local base station and then fed into the landline system, where it will be routed either to a conventional telephone or to another base station, which in turn will transmit it by radio to another cell phone. This complicated routing is handled by the switch, which is typically also used for monitoring and billing. The switch—the heart of a conventional telephone system—had to be modified for wireless to handle the added complexity of the cellular architecture.

The radio and telephone technologies on which cellular systems are based each claim a distinct commercial and engineering tradition, and the segment of the radio industry from which cellular derives is even more distinctive. The original model for cellular was the two-way radio mounted in police cars, fire engines, and taxi cabs. The radios were produced by large, sophisticated companies that specialized in radio technology. The customers were a multitude of small, dispersed organizations for whom the radio was an accessory to their mission or expertise rather than a central component. Radio engineers had a reputation in the industry as cowboys: their knowledge was empirical, ad hoc, hands-on. They jiggled the system in the field until it worked. Signal quality was often indifferent, fading in and out; communications were frequently interrupted and lost; and none of this seemed to bother the end users.

Telephone equipment producers were also large and technically sophisticated, but the customers for their equipment were large and sophisticated companies too. Indeed, the equipment producers were often wholly-owned subsidiaries of their customers. Western Electric produced equipment for AT&T, for example; Alcatel, for France Telecom. In the telephone equipment industry, quality was an obsession. The dial tone must always be present when the end user picked up the phone; calls in progress must be crystal clear ("You sound as though you're right next door!") and must never be lost. The key component of landline telephone systems was the switch, and switching technology involved meticulous and fully documented software code.

The companies that pioneered cellular typically came from either the radio or the telephone side of the business. Of the firms we studied, only the two Scandinavian companies, Ericsson and Nokia, had been in both businesses prior to entering the cellular industry. AT&T was a telephone company. Motorola and Matsushita were radio companies. Each faced the major challenge of finding a partner who understood the other side of the technology and then learning to work intimately with that partner to create the new product. Not an easy task. The cultural differences between radio and telephone engineering were deep-rooted. In our interviews, Ericsson, despite having always had internal divisions dealing with both technologies, was the most vociferous of all the companies about the difficulties of merging these two industrial cultures.

Blue Jeans

The centerpiece of the blue jeans case study was Levi Strauss and Co., which started out as a manufacturer of workmen's blue jeans. "Levi's" remains the company's defining product, and it has dominated the market for blue jeans in a way that almost no other company anywhere—certainly no other clothing company—dominates its product market. While jeans are now produced throughout the world and the Levi's brand has lost some of its allure, Levi Strauss is still one of the world's largest producers, and its product remains the point of reference for the entire industry. Other brands of jeans are virtually never purchased without some thought to Levi's as an alternative.

In the United States, blue jeans are the standard work clothing. Levi's are manufactured out of blue denim fabric, with patented reinforcing copper rivets. They are produced in very large volume and have been sold in a limited number of standard cuts and styles since they were first introduced by Levi Strauss in San Francisco in 1873. Levi's are the prototypical commodity of American mass consumption, the Model T of the garment industry. Clothing production is notoriously difficult to mechanize, but the cutting and assembly of jeans is as close to assembly-line production as can be found in the outer garment industry.

Historically, blue jeans have had very little fashion content. This changed dramatically in the early 1970s, propelled by the sudden popularity of American-made jeans in Europe. Levi Strauss moved to take advantage of this trend by selling its Levi's products abroad for two and three times the retail price they commanded in the United States. The spread between European prices and costs created enormous profits that attracted local producers into the industry. To compete with the cachet of American-made jeans, these new entrants sought to stylize their garments, differentiating the product through new cuts, finishes, and variations upon the standard dark-blue denim. These fashions were then imported into the United States in the early 1980s, invading Levi's home market. Levi Strauss was forced to defend its brand by adopting many of the European fashions and, ultimately, to preempt the Europeans by introducing innovations of its own. This involved something of a revolution in the ethos of a company which, for the first century of its existence, had never thought of itself as a fashion company at all. By the time we conducted our interviews in 1995, the new orientation was well established.

The focus in blue jeans fashion, almost from the beginning and certainly in recent years, has been the finishing process and the way this affects the look and "hand," or feel, of the garment. The driver here is the used clothing market. Manufacturers attempt to create the look, feel, and comfort of worn jeans. The basic technology involves laundering the garment to soften the texture of the fabric. Washing also shrinks the jeans, altering the fit, and changes the color in ways that are not easily produced by chemicals and dyes. A further range of effects is produced by washing in combination with different chemicals.

The finished garment is typically abraded as well. The standard abrading technique is to wash the jeans with "stones" or pumice. A typical jeans laundry thus consists of banks of industrial washing machines which are opened periodically to disgorge dozens of pairs of pants and pounds upon pounds of the rocks with which they have been washed. Jeans are now also abraded mechanically with sandpaper, or are sandblasted in order to produce the lines and creases of used garments. There is continual experimentation with new techniques, both to produce effects already achieved in other ways and to create new effects. In the pursuit of a fashion edge, manufacturers expend as much as 80 percent of the life of the garment during the finishing process.

These new finishing techniques have led to a cascade of changes in cooperating industries. Textiles have been redesigned to better withstand the extensive abrasion. Washing machines have been redesigned to survive the abuse of stone washing. They are also equipped with computer controls that can adjust the machine to different kinds of stones. Continuing changes in raw materials and equipment have the incidental effect of subtle and not so subtle changes in the look and feel of the finished garment; this in turn becomes a new fashion element that the company may try to reproduce in its other laundries.

Thus, the conversion of Levi Strauss from a manufacturing company to a fashion house—and the development and evolution of fashion jeans more broadly—involved crossing the boundaries that separated manufacturing from style and design and from the previously distinct industries of textiles, laundering and finishing, and washing machines. In many ways the cultures of these industries were as different as the cultures of telephone and radio. Levi's old garment-assembly operations and the design and manufacture of washing machines were highly structured and engineered, although based of course on quite different technologies. Both style and finishing tended to be much more free-wheeling, ad hoc, intuitive, or empirical, although the kind of intuition involved in producing new finishing effects was very different from the intuition involved in fashion.

A further dimension of the emergent fashion jean industry involved advertising and merchandising. Blue jeans are part of mass culture, and the media and advertising play a central role in their appeal. But the relationship between the product and the media is much more complex than in most industries because advertising is itself a part of the mass culture out of which fashion grows. The result is an unusual interaction between the company, the advertising industry, and other vehicles of popular culture.

Medical Devices

Our interviews in this industry involved a diverse set of companies and products. But the centerpiece was Aspect Medical Systems, founded in 1987 to exploit a technique for extracting information from electrical impulses emitted by the organs of the human body. The technique reduces these complex signals to a single numerical index, the Bispectral Index (BIS). The firm was founded on the premise that the BIS could be useful in the diagnosis and treatment of various medical conditions. We interviewed Aspect every few months over the course of a two-year period.

We also conducted interviews in five other companies. Among these was Chiron, one of the most prominent of the first generation of U.S. biotechnology companies founded during the late 1970s and early 80s. At Chiron we focused on a DNA-based diagnostic technology used to measure the presence of viral DNA or RNA in blood or plasma. Chiron's technology allows the quantification of viral load, in contrast to the more common tests for the presence of viruses that give a binary (positive or negative) response.

Both Aspect and Chiron were founded by academics, and the companies considered their roots in the scholarly community to be a key strength. Aspect was founded by Nassib Chamoun, a Harvard Ph.D. who had developed the company's core technology in his doctoral dissertation. Chiron was founded by three professors in the San Francisco Bay area who sought to use the emerging tools and techniques of biotechnology to develop new medical products. The particular DNA-based diagnostic technology that was the focus of our research at Chiron—called branched-DNA or bDNA—had actually been acquired through a complex series of mergers and acquisitions involving several other companies, but considerable research was being conducted in the company's own laboratories to improve certain properties of the viral load test and make it more competitive with alternative measurement technologies.

Precisely because they originated in academic science, the technologies developed at both Aspect and Chiron were at the outset far removed from commercial viability. Product development involved breaking free of the confines of the research community to find a use for the new discoveries. And that in turn depended on understanding and coming to terms with the clinical practice of medicine. This was actually a two-step process. First, the firms had to find a medical problem to which their technology offered a solution. Then they had to somehow design a product that fit into the clinical practices and procedures surrounding that medical problem.

Aspect investigated several different human organs before settling on the brain as a promising target. From among the many medical issues associated with the brain, the company then chose anesthesiology as its focus. Aspect next had to persuade key members of the anesthesiology profession that the clinical judgments upon which their practice was based had severe limitations. Once this need for a new technology was established, the company actually gave the machines to leading physicians for use in their day-to-day practice. The doctors were asked to calibrate the machine's measurements of the effectiveness of anesthesia against their own clinical judgments. Finally, before bringing the product to market, the company had to study the operating room itself, in order to design a device that would fit comfortably into a space that was already overcrowded with people and machines.

Chiron went through a very similar process. First, it had to identify a disease in which its bDNA technology was important for determining treatment. This is not the case for all ailments. There are, for example, large variations in the level of mycobacterium tuberculosis in the blood among cases of tuberculosis, and the bDNA technology can measure these; but the prescribed treatment for the disease does not vary with this indicator. New AIDS treatments, however, turned out to be very sensitive to viral load, and this became a promising domain for the application of Chiron's technology. Once again, the device was given to a group of lead practitioners who were asked to calibrate the measurements against their clinical judgments about optimal treatment. Thus at Chiron, as at Aspect, a tight link was established between the new scientific technologies and medical practice in the particular areas in which the products were first applied. In both cases, it was only by opening up the boundaries between the laboratory and the examining or operating room that such a link could be created.

The other medical equipment companies we interviewed were much more established and consequently less concerned with moving beyond their own boundaries. But they were, as a result, prisoners of the boundaries that had developed around their original technologies, and they found it very difficult to break into new areas. Hewlett-Packard, for example, had been trying to extend its market from cardiology imaging to other kinds of medical imaging, but, as we will see, it was able to do so only by accident—through a strategic alliance with Philips Medical Systems that had been organized for a completely different purpose.

Integration during Product Design and Manufacturing

Integration was central in each of our three cases, but there were at least two qualitatively different processes at work.

One involved integration among technical specialties and across the boundaries of the different firms and organizational units involved in the design and production process. The second type of integration involved the boundaries between producers and final consumers.

In the first type, the basic tasks seemed to be to identify the various units that needed to cooperate, to give them a goal, and then to remove any organizational barriers to collaboration. The goals were often only vaguely specified: design a commercially viable product, or a product that is technically feasible, or—in the case of fashion jeans—a product that is just interesting and original. The removal of internal obstacles to successful collaboration was often more complicated.

In cell phones, for example, the particular strategy varied with the company and its history. Among the companies we visited, AT&T was perhaps the most formally structured; in outward appearance, at least, it was the classic hierarchical bureaucracy. The initial development of cell phone technology took place at Bell Labs, a sheltered enclave within AT&T that enjoyed the research ethos of an academic laboratory. Bell Labs was insulated from commercial pressures and hospitable to collaboration among different scientific and engineering disciplines.

AT&T's competitor, Motorola, attacked the problem of integration by giving one of its prospective clients—a Japanese cellular company with a reputation for exacting standards—direct access to its development engineers. The customer's technicians got to know the Motorola engineers working on the feature of the system that particularly concerned them, and they were able to call them up directly without passing through an organizational gatekeeper.

Nokia provided similar access to its clients, but in this case access was mediated by the company's sales staff. The character of Nokia's original cellular organization is captured in the comment from one of our respondents in the handset division: "The business was much smaller [than it is today]. Product managers were drawn from R&D and were known as good phone makers, so there was a technology push. There was no marketing. The sales guy would see some competitor's product with better or different features, and they would come in and say we want this or that. And we would redesign the product in the middle of the project."

To solve the problem of production integration at Levi's, the company collected engineers from its leading laundries and textile suppliers and had them travel abroad with its own designers to observe fashion trends and participate actively in the meetings surrounding Levi's new collections.

At both Aspect and Chiron, early versions of their products—the brain activity monitor in the case of Aspect and the chemical assays and diagnostics in the case of Chiron—were supplied directly to chosen doctors who became, in effect, members of the design team. One of the problems for young companies like these is that they do not know where their innovations will be commercially viable, and hence they must continually develop new relationships with clinicians. Older companies, by contrast, typically specialize in one medical area, where longstanding relationships with clinicians guide product development; innovations in these firms tend to be more market driven. One of the rationales for mergers between biotechnology start-ups and established pharmaceutical firms is to marry the marketing expertise of the latter with the creativity of the former.

At the time of our interviews, Chiron had developed a strategic alliance with a large company, Daiichi Pure Chemicals, which served as its sales representative in Japan. Relative to Chiron, Daiichi appeared to be much more driven by the market than by research and development and had the kind of clinical connections in Japan that Chiron lacked in the United States. Daiichi tended to develop new products to treat diseases for which it already had a track record, such as liver diseases, because its existing products gave it good contacts with the market.

The partnership between Chiron and Daiichi did not flourish. Chiron attributed marketing failures to a lack of commitment on the part of its partner, while Daiichi blamed the problem on inconsistency of the viral load test results from sample to sample. But Chiron never heard this message because of the arm's-length relationship it had established with Daiichi. Ironically, it was precisely in the domain of consistency from test to test that Chiron's product was superior to that of its chief competitor in the marketplace, a different DNA-based product employing polymerase chain reaction (PCR) technology. The main advantage of this competitor was its greater sensitivity to the presence of virus; consequently, Chiron's research effort had been devoted not to the problem of consistency of viral load measurements but rather to the problem of improving the sensitivity of its test.

Despite the many attempts of the companies we studied to reduce organizational boundaries during the production stage, success was often elusive. At Levi Strauss, a particular problem that demanded an organizational solution was how to reproduce the finishing effects developed in one laundry at the numerous other laundries producing the same garment. Because finishing technology was still highly empirical, new effects were sometimes achieved inadvertently, and it was not always easy to identify the factors involved in creating any given effect or the obstacles to reproducing it at another particular location, given the variations in machinery, water, and other ancillary inputs at different laundries. One of Levi's chief engineers proposed monthly meetings of the lead engineers from each of the laundries as a way of addressing this problem. But, as we will see, collaboration at these meetings was inhibited by Levi's long-standing practice of pitting its different laundries against one another in a competition to drive down costs.

Integration between Producer and Final Consumer

Several of our case studies prominently featured attempts to overcome barriers between producers and consumers. For the most part, these efforts differed significantly from those aimed at removing organizational barriers within and among producers. The products we studied were almost all produced for a mass market in which it was difficult to identify a single representative consumer. In the management literature and in the popular press, a commonly prescribed solution to this problem is to set up a focus group. But our respondents were very skeptical of focus groups, basically because the interesting products were so new and so foreign to consumers that a focus group could not readily imagine how the products would be of use.

The approach adopted by our companies was for the designers to observe consumers themselves and then to discuss and debate the implications of what they had observed for the different design alternatives. In the very early stages of a new product, this meant observing consumers in settings where there was no product at all. In later stages, the design team would try to figure out, by paying attention to the way consumers treated early versions of the product, what changes should be introduced subsequently. In cell phones, the move toward portability and miniaturization emerged from observations of how consumers were using bulky, awkward car-mounted phones.

In jeans, designers spent a considerable amount of time visiting used clothing stores, watching and listening to shoppers as they picked over the racks. Levi's also took teams of designers and even engineers on trips abroad to observe consumers in Italy, who were thought to be particularly fashion-conscious. Levi's set up its own retail outlets, so that specially trained salesmen or their own designers could interact directly with customers and pick up comments and observations.

Matsushita in cellular and Oticon, a Danish producer of hearing aids we visited, also owned retail outlets for the primary purpose of gathering customer feedback; the volume of sales in these outlets was trivial. An extreme version of this approach was a Japanese company, Onward Kashiyama, which, when it decided to enter the market for nautical sports clothes, developed an entire marine resort complex, where it featured its clothing collection along with a complete vacation package that included a luxury hotel, fine cuisine, and high-end sporting equipment.

One very important side-effect of this attempt to overcome the boundary between the consumer and producer was unanticipated. It turned out that discussions about consumers helped to break down barriers between different constituents of the producer team and build rapport among them. Apparently, having a third party as the target of conversation made it much easier for members of the different engineering communities to unite and resolve their own boundary issues.

Managing Boundaries, Not Dismantling Them

Although much of management's attention in product development is aimed at opening borders so that communication can occur across them, we also observed movement in the other direction. At certain times and in certain places, management was also concerned with *closing* borders that previously had been open and with erecting new barriers within their own organization and between their company and the rest of the world.

The most striking example of the role of boundary management in corporate integration efforts emerged in the cellular case. Each of the five companies we visited embarked on the cellular business with quite open, loose organizational structures for product development, in which people interacted easily with others in the group and with outside customers as well. But over time, each of the companies came to impose much stricter boundaries between their internal divisions and between the company and the outside world. These transitions all occurred in an interval between the late 1980s and early 1990s, in each case in response to a severe financial crisis.

The most dramatic reorganization took place at AT&T. Cellular was moved from Bell Labs into a separate business unit that was subject to the conventional AT&T bureaucratic practices and hierarchy. None of the other companies ever had a sheltered environment like Bell Labs in which to start the development of cellular. Most of them began by assembling groups of engineers into newly created but poorly defined organizational entities, where they worked in teams with an ambiguous division of labor and sometimes confused lines of authority. Like AT&T, however, they all ended up adopting more formal, systematic decisionmaking processes and creating better defined organizational structures in which to house the cellular business.

The new procedures and structures varied significantly from one company to another. The transition was least pronounced at Nokia and Motorola, where an effort was made to preserve at least some aspects of the original, more informal approach. Nevertheless, all of the companies moved in the same direction, toward more clearly delineated boundaries and stricter policing of them. But the new boundaries turned out to be much more contingent than anticipated, and the companies were forced to reevaluate and revise them over time.

In order to establish these boundaries, the companies wanted to divide their cellular systems into discrete, clearly defined components. Each component could then be assigned to a separate division of the organization (or a subdivision within the cellular unit). The companies also wanted to be able to withdraw from certain parts of the cellular system or to purchase them from external suppliers. The cellular switch posed a recurring problem in this regard. Neither Motorola nor Matsushita, both of them originally radio companies, had ever produced a telephone switch in-house. Motorola tried several different solutions to the problem of integrating switching technology, none of which were particularly successful. In one case they developed a strategic alliance with a leading non-U.S. company, but that collaboration failed. Matsushita ultimately decided to exit the infrastructure side of the business and concentrate on handsets, in part because of its inability to find a suitable switching partner.

The three companies that did produce switches handled the relationship with the rest of the system in different ways. At Nokia the cellular division purchased switches from other parts of the company and modified them internally. At both Ericsson and AT&T, the cellular business unit was forced to rely entirely on an independent, self-contained unit elsewhere in the company for the switch.

In Europe the development of the GSM digital standard

facilitated the task of dividing the cellular system into separable components that could be allocated to different units. The GSM standard codified the interfaces between the components, which in principle enabled customers to combine components purchased from different suppliers. But whenever a problem emerged in these hybrid systems, diagnosis and correction turned out to be difficult or impossible. The components interacted in unexpected ways. Other system interdependencies were revealed by the drive to reduce the size of the cellular telephone and make it more portable. Miniaturization required that functions previously housed inside the phone itself had to be moved out into the infrastructure. Evidently the boundaries within the system were less well-defined and less stable than the new organization charts implied. More integration across boundaries was necessary than had been anticipated, and the boundaries themselves had to be revised as products evolved.

The boundary management pattern we observed in the cellular companies also emerged at Aspect Medical Systems. Here, too, in the early stages of development the border between the company and the customer was wide open, and company personnel were encouraged to interact with clinicians and even to offer them free use of the equipment. The sales function was thus not really distinguishable from other activities, and the company's senior officers were particularly active in talking to clinicians about their product's innovations and in recruiting physicians to experiment with the devices the company was developing.

When Aspect developed its second-generation product, however, a separate sales force was created to deal with the marketplace, and direct contacts between potential customers and other employees were blocked. A legal consideration in this decision grew out of the need to comply with FDA restrictions on what claims a company could legitimately make for its product in the marketplace. But the main rationale for the move was that trained sales people would be better able to judge the seriousness of clients' interest and to identify those practitioners whose willingness to experiment with the equipment could help the company calibrate its machine with clinical practice.

In a related move, Aspect abandoned its practice of providing free equipment, arguing that a nominal charge—still well below cost—would help to screen out physicians who would not actually use the equipment. A professional sales force could also identify those key anesthesiologists whose influence over their colleagues might help establish Aspect's device as the gold standard in the profession.

The company discussed hiring a vendor firm instead of creating its own sales organization, but it rejected this alternative because of the need for close interaction between the sales force and the product development organization within the company. In selecting members of its sales team, Aspect recruited a number of operating room nurses—practitioners who had first-hand experience with the target customer and who understood the environment in which those clinicians operated.

Boundary management took a different form in the garment industry. There, the focus was on managing boundaries to allow the free flow of ideas while limiting leaks of trade secrets to competitors. This issue was of particular concern in the production of blue jeans, where rapidly evolving finishing technologies were regarded as a key stimulus to creativity and a critical source of competitive advantage. But this exposure could also put one at a competitive disadvantage if rival companies stole one's ideas. Consequently, there was an ongoing debate in the industry about exactly how much and what kind of interaction with other companies was necessary to maintain a creative edge. The companies in our case studies chose radically different solutions to this problem, as we will see, and they debated these differences at length in our interviews.

The Problem of Language and Vocabulary

For all the talk about integration across boundaries in the literature and in our own interviews, our respondents were much more comfortable with—and much better at talking about—a world in which boundaries were well defined and well policed than a world in which communication was free and open. Their unease is difficult to document, but it is suggested by the way they explained and justified their choice of strategies. The cellular companies' discussion of their transition from informal to more formal organizational structures beginning in the late 1980s is a case in point.

Ericsson and AT&T, the two companies which introduced the sharpest boundaries at that time, made no attempt to justify the change in organizational structure at all. By contrast, the companies where the reorganization was less radical and preserved more of the original integration strained to explain what they had done. Motorola, borrowing directly from AT&T, had installed a powerful project manager to mediate relationships with customers but then had proceeded to limit his authority. The employees who spoke with us attributed this softening to internal politics and the resistance of people who were accustomed to the old way of doing things. At Nokia, where even after the transition the procedures tended to be much less rigid and bureaucratic than at Ericsson, employees explained the contrast in terms of the differences between Swedish and Finnish "culture." The fact is that at both Motorola and Nokia, management had a strong business rationale for the approach that was taken, but our respondents were never willing or able to fully articulate what that justification was.

The difficulties of talking about integration were thus reflected more in the tone and tenor of the interviews than in their specific content. But, for us, this was a turning point in our understanding of the phenomenon we were observing. We came to believe that the bias we detected in these interviews was not really just about the organizational boundaries themselves. It was more fundamental than that—the product of a particular way of thinking that grew out of our respondents' training. That training reflected an analytical approach to the overall task of product development and to the roles of managers and engineers in this process. The rationale for opening borders, and for the things that happen when one does, involved a very different approach to management, one which we call *interpretation*. This was the aspect of their activities that our respondents seemed to have the most difficulty discussing. It is not that they were unaware of the need for a process—or a way of thinking and talking—that would improve integration both within the company and without. But the terms available to them for discussing this missing dimension seemed superficial at best. In the next chapter, we will expand upon this difficulty and upon the critical differences between analytical and interpretive thinking in product design and in management more broadly.

WHERE DO PROBLEMS COME FROM?

2

The engineers and managers in our case studies almost always described the development and design of new products in terms of problem-solving. As one of the people we interviewed put it, "Design is problem solving! It's generic problem solving." But the respondents in our case studies were also engaged in activities that did not readily fit within this problem-solving framework. While they had much to say about the analytical approach to the task at hand, they said much less about where the problems came from in the first place.

Most of the designers we interviewed recognized that a process for generating not just solutions but the problems themselves could not be shoe-horned into the problem-solving format. Some said so quite explicitly and self-consciously, while others displayed an implicit awareness of this in practice. But they lacked a vocabulary and a conceptual framework with which to talk about problem-eliciting activities, and so they usually fell back upon a terminology borrowed from analysis and rational decision-making. This default vocabulary made it difficult for them to distinguish between the two kinds of activities and to act deliberately and purposively to improve performance along the nonanalytical dimension.

The Ubiquity of Problem Solving

Among the designers we interviewed who used an analytical or problem-solving approach to the task of new product development, the ultimate goal was to arrive quickly at a fully specified design that could be produced economically and brought to market rapidly. The key to doing so was to work through a chain of decisions. The first decision was to establish clear objectives for the new product. Typically this involved identifying the target market segment and trying, more or less systematically, to determine the customer's wants or needs. Next, the main constraints on the project had to be established—the target timeframe for product introduction, the budget, the plans of competitors, and so on—and the available resources assembled.

If, as was usually the case, the development project was too large and complicated to be undertaken by a single individual, it would then be partitioned into discrete subtasks, each assigned to the appropriate expert. The component parts of the problem would be solved by these experts, and the resulting pieces would be brought together into the final product, generally with some additional attempt to optimize both the product itself and the process by which it would be produced.

Among the engineers we interviewed, the prominence given to problem solving during product development was to be expected. Problem solving is central to the professional identity of engineers, and it is the approach to engineering that is taught to students. Recent research by academics studying product development has been directed at refining this approach and developing new tools for implementing it.[1] But the basic sequence prescribed for use in product design is quite general. Would-be practitioners learn to begin by making a sharp distinction between ends and means—between the goal they are trying to achieve and the resources available for achieving it. Their next step is to specify a causal model connecting the means to the ends. Finally, they are taught to optimize—that is, to solve the causal model so as to maximize the degree to which the goal is achieved, given the constraints on resources.

When there are multiple, possibly conflicting, goals, they are taught to identify the trade-offs among them and to look for solutions that achieve acceptable performance with respect to each goal at minimum cost. Where the problem is too complex to be solved directly, it is broken down into independent components, for each of which a solution is possible. When a component of the problem cannot be solved directly, the optimum is approached through iteration.

Many of the design issues that emerged in our product-development case studies were indeed best understood as problems to be solved. For example, at Lutron, the lighting controls company, a key issue from the outset was the protrusion of the light-dimmer box from the wall. This design allows heat generated in the dimming process to dissipate, but it is at odds with the aesthetic of interior design, which dictates that light switches must be flush with the wall. As Lutron worked through successive iterations in solving the dimmer-box protrusion problem, each generation of light switch fit a little more snugly against the wall.

Another long-standing issue facing Lutron was the need for lighting between the time that a person hit the switch to turn off a fixture and the time that she actually reached her bed or other destination across the room. Yet a third issue was the search for a means to centrally control all the lighting in the house. As with the protrusion of the dimmer box, Lutron viewed each of these issues as a problem to be solved, and the genealogy of the company's products could be viewed as iterations on a solution. For example, a portable infrared dimming wand was developed that a person could aim at the wall fixture to turn off the light after she got into bed. One of Lutron's latest products, a portable radio device that controls lighting throughout the house, could solve both problems at the same time.

The evolution of the cell phone system can be understood as an attempt to solve two problems: the scarcity of radio frequencies and hence the need to squeeze as many calls as possible into a given frequency bandwidth; and the desire to reduce the handset in size so as to maximize its portability. The significance of the latter can be seen in successive generations of cell phones, each one of which is smaller, lighter, and more compact than the last. The scarcity issue was understood in terms of a classic trade-off between quality and quantity; if calls are too closely spaced, either geographically or along the radio spectrum, they interfere with one another, making it difficult or impossible to understand the messages being transmitted. The choice of where to locate on the quantity-quality continuum brought to the fore the conflict between the telephone culture, with its emphasis on quality, and the freewheeling, cowboy culture of radio. The competing digital technologies of Time Division Multiple Access (TDMA) and Code Division Multiple Access (CDMA) represented two different solutions to a well-defined problem: how to increase the number of calls of a given quality that could utilize the same set of frequencies simultaneously.

Even in the case of fashion jeans, which one might think would be most resistant to a problem-solving approach, the product's evolution can be understood in these terms. The drive to reproduce the look and feel of worn jeans generates a series of subproblems, for each of which the industry devised and analyzed alternative strategies. At the time of our interviews, for example, one company we visited was concentrating on reproducing the "moustaches" (the wear lines radiating out from the crotch) through the use of hand-held electric sanders—clearly a high-fashion "problem" crying out for solution.

The Limitations of Problem Solving

But not all activity that takes place in product development fits neatly into this problem-solving framework. Style is particularly difficult to understand in these terms. Even the most analytical engineers we interviewed recognized the desirability of designing products with a distinctive look and feel, but the search for an attractive look and feel was not readily perceived as the solution to a problem. Attempts to squeeze it into that format usually come off as sounding absurd.

For example, the Nobel Prize–winning economist Herbert Simon argued that style in architecture is the result of the fact that the problem of optimizing the design of a building is too complex to be "solved" all at once. The design is thus arrived at sequentially, and for that reason the outcome will depend on where one begins. Some architects, Simon claimed, start at the outside and work in; others start at the inside and work out. And these different starting points impart a distinctive style to the buildings those architects produce.[2] In Simon's view, style occurs by default. But in talking to engineers about their work, we quickly learned that style by default was definitely not what they were striving to impart to the products they produced.

The very notion of design as problem solving seems to

suggest another dimension within the innovative process. It raises the question of how the problems that are to be solved come to be defined at the outset. Consumers or customers or clients who have not yet imagined a product do not know what they want, and engineers are not sure what they can build. At least in the early stages of product development, it simply is not possible to arrive at a clear, unambiguous set of objectives for the project, no matter how carefully one listens to the customer's voice. We encountered many such situations in our case studies.

In the early years of mobile telephones, for example, none of the leading manufacturers knew for certain how the new technology would be used by consumers. The product was totally new. The closest analogs were the two-way radios used by police and emergency services, taxi fleets, truckers, and the like. Many engineers believed that the mobile phone would remain a car-mounted device, used primarily by people in mobile professions—salespeople, for example, or appliance repairmen. Almost no one imagined the extent to which ordinary consumers would quickly demand mobile phone equipment.

But the way consumers used these mobile telephones—carrying them back and forth from their automobiles to meetings, or into their homes to charge the battery—pointed away from the concept of "car phones" and toward the idea of portable, hand-carried "cell phones," with their progressively lighter and more compact designs. Only after seeing how consumers treated the initial products were engineers able to envisage a hand-held instrument that could be used while walking down the street or in the airport.

Today, of course, the images that drive the market are the business executive who cannot afford to be out of touch with his office, the teenager who cannot wait to talk to his friends, or the grandma-on-the-go. The email, text messaging, and Internet services that are now being built into the instrument did not even exist when the product was initially brought to market.

When the founders of Aspect Medical first sought to commercialize the technology they had developed to monitor and interpret electrical signals from human organs, they had the idea of using it for diagnosis and treatment of a variety of medical conditions. Eventually they limited their device to monitoring the impact of anesthesia on brain activity, but only after an earlier plan to develop a heart monitoring system had been abandoned. Moreover, the decision to develop the anesthesia monitoring device was not made in response to an explicit demand for such an instrument. On the contrary, an important part of product development was to persuade anesthesiologists of the value of a device they had previously been unaware they needed.

These examples are not unusual. In many other industries, innovations can be identified that did not, at least initially, address a particular need or problem, or for which the problem became apparent only after the product was in use. In such cases, the product developer frequently starts out without really knowing what she is trying to create. The uncertainty surrounding the developer's activities at this point cannot be described analytically. In analysis, uncertainty is treated in terms of probabilities. The analyst seeks to identify the possible outcomes, attaches a probability to each one, and then weights each outcome by its probability in order to calculate the expected payoff. But the kind of uncertainty involved in the design of new products is more often a *radical* uncertainty.

Radical uncertainty is not simply an inability to predict which of several possible configurations of the product will turn out to be the preferred one, or which segment of the market will yield the highest profit margins. In these situations the world appears so complex and uncertain that not even the possible outcomes are known. And in the absence of a specified outcome in the form of a well-defined product, it is unclear how to break the problem up into a set of separable parts that can be assigned to different specialists. Indeed, it is not even clear what those specialties should be.

Most of the respondents in our case studies were conscious of this uncertain dimension in design, and they sought to manage it in a deliberate and self-conscious way, as something that was distinct from problem-solving activity. They recognized that something else was going on, but they did not have a good way to talk about it. When they spoke about it experientially, they used homey expressions to characterize what they were doing. "You have to kiss a lot of frogs" cropped up repeatedly in our interviews with engineers. This phrase made innovation seem like a random process, one that was haphazard, ad hoc, a matter of trial and error, and—as the reference to the fairy tale prince suggests—mysterious and perhaps a little magical, too.

When respondents tried to talk about design more reflectively, they fell back on clichés. In several companies, they made a distinction between two kinds of designers: the technical problem-solvers and the "creative" or "big-think" people. Company managers talked about the proper mix of these two types and the perpetual problem of getting them to relate to one another. Yet overall, the attitude of our respondents appeared to be disassociated and even contradictory. They were uncomfortable with the more speculative, open-ended part of the innovative process and wanted to squeeze it back into a problem-solving format, but they also recognized on some level that this was neither possible nor desirable.

The most coherent effort available today to organize the innovative process and manage it in analytical terms is contained in a family of international quality management standards called ISO 9000. ISO 9000 was developed and is maintained by the International Organization for Standardization (ISO), a network of national standards institutes from 148 countries working in partnership with international organizations, governments, businesses, and consumer representatives. ISO publishes voluntary technical standards covering almost every sector and function of industry. ISO 9000 is generally concerned with how organizations should manage their processes and activities, and it includes a set of standards and procedures for the organization of product development. These essentially divide the process into a series of stages and create "gates" that control movement from one stage to the next. The procedures specify strict criteria that must be met at each review stage and also which parts of the company must participate. Thus, the earliest stage entails a very preliminary sketch of a product idea, with only a ballpark cost estimate for development and a single price point. At later stages, the manufacturing and purchasing departments are drawn into the process and must sign off on the design before it can move forward.

Virtually everyone with whom we talked in our interviews was familiar with the ISO 9000 standards, and some of them had actually instituted modified versions of these procedures in their own companies. But everybody was also skeptical about their value, and several were strongly opposed to them. When it came to actually specifying what the problem with these standards was, however, our respondents were less articulate. The best that people could do to pin down their skepticism was to complain that ISO 9000 was too bureaucratic. But nobody seemed able to articulate how, exactly, it was too bureaucratic, or what aspect of the innovation process was left out, or what the nature of the excluded process was that they felt ought to have been captured.

Tacit recognition of this missing dimension manifested itself in considerable skepticism not only about ISO 9000 but about *any* efforts to systematize innovation. Representative, and for us canonical, of this stance was the comment of Lutron's founder, Joel Spira, during a discussion of the set of design axioms developed by the noted MIT mechanical engineering professor Nam Suh.[3] Suh's first axiom is to choose a design that can be broken down into a series of separable components; that is, into problems that can be solved independently of one another. An example of a perfect design in these terms is the church key, with a can opener at one end and a bottle opener at the other. Spira remarked that Nam Suh is exactly right on this score, but then he added a key qualification: "This is the most basic principle but it is not operational . . . The real problem is to envisage a solution." In other words, how do you divide the whole into parts if you do not first know what the whole is?

But with many managers this skepticism coexisted with a powerful nostalgia for an analytical approach that they themselves were unable (and in the case of ISO 9000, unwilling) to apply. This point was driven home to us on a three-day trip to the San Francisco Bay area, during which we alternated between interviews with biotechnology companies and with Levi Strauss executives. After describing how their laundries developed and disseminated the finishing effects that drove style in blue jeans—a process involving a lot of ad hoc experimentation, closely akin to kissing frogs—one of the executives talked about his plans in the future to cross-train his jeans designers in chemical engineering. "Then we will do it," he said, "just like they do in biotech." But what we actually learned in our biotechnology interviews was that *they* were doing it just like they do in blue jeans! The chemists were producing new assays and giving them to commercial labs to play around with and see what they could discover in terms of new uses, just as the laundries were playing around with different ways of washing and abrading denim.

The tendency of many of our respondents to side-step the conflicts between the design process as actually practiced and the analytical approach to problem solving is also present in the notion of the "heavyweight" manager. This term was introduced into the scholarly literature by Kim B. Clark, Dean of the Harvard Business School, and Takahiro Fujimoto in their book about design and development in the automobile industry, *Product Development Performance*.[4] The authors focus on integration as the chief organizational problem that design and product development teams have to solve. In the kind of organizational structure that Clark and Fujimoto strongly endorse, authority is concentrated in one person, who develops the initial design and makes all of the critical decisions about its execution.

The same basic approach appears in many different forms and under different names, especially in computer programming, an industry haunted by the impossibility of breaking up code writing into separable components. One major problem is that bugs emerge when the components are put together in a "build" and allowed to interact with one another. This problem is compounded when code becomes too elaborate and cumbersome for the tasks it was intended to perform. The ideal solution, proposed by Frederick P. Brooks in his classic book on software engineering, *The Mythical Man-Month*, is to have one person do the whole thing: lay out the basic architecture, design the system, and write the code.[5] The chief works with a team and there is a division of labor of sorts, but the rest of the team essentially clears the decks so that the chief can do his thing. They bring him the tools he needs—background material and code from the library—and they do the testing. They supply coffee, breakfast, lunch, and dinner when necessary—whatever it takes to finish the job.

The image of the heavyweight manager cropped up in our study of the apparel industry, in an interview with Camaïeu, a French retail chain selling women's undergarments and outerwear. Camaïeu's approach is to collect a series of designs from a variety of different sources, produce them in small lots, and display them in its test stores. The designs that sell are then reordered in volume and used to stock its other outlets. The result is a collection which, in contrast to other retailers (the Gap for example, or virtually any collection in a department store) has no coherence. It is an approach that may work in France, where women have strong personal tastes and a good deal of self-confidence about style; but Camaïeu executives recognized that it would be much more problematic in the United States. The only real alternative in their eyes was to have a strong executive who designed the whole collection.

As a matter of fact, there is another alternative that was used by all of the other garment firms that we visited: design teams. They worked out the new collections in common, picking a set of themes and exploring the implications in a series of conversations around sketches and prototypes. Then they left the individual members to design the separate parts of the collection, trusting them to work within the ethos that the team had generated as a group.

At Levi Strauss (and in many other garment companies)

an important feature of this team-building process was the shopping trips that designers and producers took to key fashion centers like Milan, where they spent their days not so much buying (although they did buy) as watching people in the streets and listening to them in the stores while they looked at merchandise and tried on clothing. They then returned to their hotel at night and discussed with other team members what they had seen and what it might imply for the collection they were going to develop when they returned home.

Other designers at Levi's spent their time listening to radio stations, visiting clubs, and shopping at stores frequented by the trend-setters in their assigned segment of the market. They then returned "home" to discuss what they had seen with designers following other market segments. Frequently, these designers also joined the international shopping teams. The collection emerged out of these intersecting discussions. This process had a number of ramifications, but the important point here is that the ethos which emerged was a substitute for—or the moral equivalent of—the heavyweight manager. It created a group that shared a mentality. When the group then split up and the job of creating a common collection was divided into pieces that the members produced separately, the pieces had the same kind of coherence that a heavyweight manager might produce.

This and many other examples we encountered suggested one of the difficulties in characterizing the nonanalytical part of the design process: the only activity that can actually be identified and described is a conversation. Once we saw this in our case studies, we began to wonder whether it was exactly this notion of a conversation that our other respondents were also reaching for.

Consider, for example, the manager in Hewlett-Packard's medical devices division who discussed with us her efforts to stimulate ideas about manufacturing technology among her team of engineers. In order to protect its proprietary technology, the company had a closed internal structure and tight boundaries that insulated it from others in the industry, from suppliers up-stream, and even from clients outside the narrow segment of the market it served. To compensate, she told us with a smile, she took the engineering division on "technology shopping trips" to visit other plants within the company and, when she could gain access, outside.

The metaphor was homey; it played on her still somewhat unusual position as a woman heading a mostly male engineering department. It was also a curious way to describe what in analytical terms was essentially a reconnaissance mission. From an analytical perspective, in fact, the whole trip was curious. Why take the whole department? One person could have been sent out to gather the same information. The different factories they visited as a team could have been parceled out to individual members, and each factory visit, which took several person-days for the group as a whole, could have been reduced to just one.

The idea of a "technology shopping trip," however, evoked for us (if not for the participants) the image of a group of girls gossiping around the clothing racks and in the dressing room. The use of this metaphor seemed to suggest that the conversation which was stimulated by these team forays was as important to the innovation process as the "information" that was gathered. In this sense, this technology shopping trip was like the actual shopping trip which the Levi Strauss team took to Italy. If that trip had been just about buying clothes, Levi Strauss could also have saved a lot of money by sending out one person to select the purchases and bring them home.

Conversation versus Problem Solving

From our interviews, we concluded that the way in which problems come to be identified and clarified to the point where a solution can be developed is through a process of conversation among people and organizations with different backgrounds and perspectives. Sometimes the process literally is a conversation; more often, conversation is a useful metaphor for the interactions that actually occur.

A critical role for the manager is to remove the organizational barriers that would otherwise prevent these conversations from taking place. The manager's task in animating conversations across borders can be contrasted with the role of the analytical, problem-solving manager, who strives for clarity. The product specifications must be clearly defined so that the project can begin. If there is no closure, the product cannot be produced.

When asked, designers and managers will usually acknowledge the risk of choosing a set of specifications prematurely. But most of them are much more attuned to its polar opposite, the danger of *not* freezing on a particular design. They fear the paralysis of indecision more than the stillbirth of options. They try to structure projects that can yield optimal solutions in the face of potentially overwhelming uncertainty. And they can draw on an impressive array of analytical tools and techniques to help them do this.

But when the problem is to keep things moving forward *without* closure, managers have far fewer resources on which to draw. The need to keep business organizations nimble and adaptable is widely recognized, but the conceptual framework that sees in ambiguity the seeds not of paralysis but of opportunity is not nearly as well developed as the analytical apparatus we routinely use to solve problems.

If American business organizations are to be fluid as well as focused, creative as well as decisive, we need a framework that is as well-suited to the problem of managing ongoing, open-ended processes—of managing ambiguity without trying to eliminate it—as our analytical portfolio is for bringing projects to closure.

CONVERSATION, INTERPRETATION, AND AMBIGUITY

3

Our respondents clearly had trouble describing the nonanalytical dimension of the process in which they were engaged. But when they actually did characterize it in a way that seemed to fit, that activity sounded an awful lot like a conversation. And what the respondents seemed to be doing was managing that conversation. The way that new designs came to be initiated, the way that new styles emerged or trends in style were "recognized," the way that problems came to be identified and clarified to the point where a solution could be discussed was through conversations among people from different backgrounds and with different perspectives.

Communication during this conversational phase is often punctuated by misunderstandings or ambiguities; indeed, an accepted vocabulary to describe the new product may not even exist. Yet this ambiguity in the conversation is the resource out of which new ideas emerge. And something is lost if that conversation is closed off too soon.

Cell phones emerged out of a conversation between members of the radio and telephone industries; medical devices emerged out of a conversation between academic scientists and medical practitioners with clinical experience; fashion jeans emerged out of a conversation between textile companies, manufacturers, laundries, and fashion designers. In each case, the manager's role was to remove organizational barriers that would have prevented these conversations from taking place.

His role was also to remove barriers between the organization and the consumer. At the outset, the customer does not really know what he wants or needs. Those needs emerge out of interactions during which the customer and the designer together discover something new about the customer's life and how the new product might fit into it. In mass markets, the notion of a conversation is more metaphorical than literal. Designers create and market a particular version of a product and then watch consumers to see how they react to it. The product is revised in light of the way it gets used. Sometimes companies seek a surrogate for the customer in the form of focus groups or lead users. But just as often, the customer communicates to designers through practice, and the designers discuss among themselves what the implications of that practice are for the next generation of products.

Conversations between producers and consumers typically take place around particular objects. These objects are often (but not always) the focus of conversations among technical experts as well. The "concept cars" developed by leading automakers and unveiled each year at venues such as the North American International Auto Show in Detroit are an example. Paul Carlile calls these focal projects *boundary objects*.[1] But in the conversational metaphor, they might be better thought of as conversation pieces. This has particular resonance in mass markets because it is so difficult to "talk" to the customer. The customer is speaking through practice, and the designer is trying to interpret what the practice says. The conversations among designers and engineers also center on particular objects and practices; indeed, it is often hard to distinguish the actual conversations among the technical specialists from the metaphorical conversation with the marketplace in which the experts try to interpret consumer practices.

Because of the way in which conversations are focused on particular objects and practices, and because they are an exploration of different views of what is essentially the same situation, we came to see the activity in which the participants are engaged as *interpretation*. This contrasts with analysis, which entails a different kind of interaction altogether.

Interpretation is an open-ended process, ongoing in time, perhaps with a beginning but with no natural end. Unlike people engaged in problem solving, the participants in a conversation often have no idea where their discussion is going when it starts; and even if they do, the actual direction may turn out to be quite different. Indeed, in retrospect they may not be able to say exactly how the conversation evolved as it did.

In stark contrast with analysis and problem solving, interpretation plays in the space of ambiguity. When a conversation begins, the participants may have considerable difficulty even understanding one another. This is most obviously true if they speak different languages; but even when they ostensibly speak the same language, misunderstandings often arise. Sometimes the conversation breaks down altogether. Only by continuing to talk to one another can participants overcome their initial lack of comprehension, work through their early misunderstandings, and make new discoveries and new insights about one another and the situations they confront.

From this perspective, ambiguity is the critical resource out of which new ideas emerge. It is ambiguity that makes the conversation worth having, not the exchange of chunks of agreed-upon information. The cell phone emerged in the space created by the ambiguity about whether the product was a radio or a telephone; by playing with that ambiguity, the device became something that was different from either of them.

Each of these contradictory processes, analysis and interpretation, is essential to design. If issues are never clarified, if problems are never solved (or at least resolved), if decisions are never made, the product will never reach the market. But the easiest products for which to achieve this kind of closure are those that are already well defined. And those are products that almost anybody can design and produce. Novelty and originality lie in the space of ambiguity. When a firm is seeking to minimize time-to-market, when marketability depends on a particular, well-understood parameter of the product—its size, for example, or its weight—analysis is the way to go. But when a firm is launching a completely new product or seeking to differentiate its offerings from those of its competitors, interpretation is the critical, sometimes-missing dimension.

The key to understanding the difference between analysis and interpretation lies in their very different views of what is involved in human communication: the precise exchange of information, on the one hand, and open-ended, unpredictable conversation, on the other. It turns out that these differences are also at the core of a current scholarly debate about the nature of human communication and language, and a brief exposure to that debate helps shed further light on the basic analytical–interpretive dichotomy.[2]

According to one view, a language consists of a set of grammatical rules and a vocabulary. Together, the grammar and vocabulary determine meaning. The process of communication then consists of applying the rules to generate a message, on one side, and to decipher the message, on the other. Each of the parties to a conversation is in effect using the rules and vocabulary to solve a communication problem. In this view, words have unambiguous meanings and convey a clear message which requires no interpretation to be understood. It is like communicating in Morse Code.

The other view of communication is that the rules and vocabulary create a space which delimits the range of possible meanings, but that the meaning of any particular exchange is constructed through the interaction of the participants in the conversation. In this view, language itself is open, not complete. Conversation is not simply about coding and decoding messages. More often than not, the messages are ambiguous, and initially there is a good deal of confusion. How people work through the ambiguity and together construct meaning in the space created by the rules and vocabulary is a process of interpretation. And through that process the participants come to understand each other—and themselves—better than before.

The view of language as open is clarified by the Berkeley professor of linguistics George Lakoff in his critique of the classical theory of categories.[3] The nouns we use in conversation are essentially categories. The classical theory of categories—which underlies the view that communication can be reduced to problem solving—implies that a category (a noun) is closed, in the sense of having clearly defined boundaries, and that any member of the category can serve to exemplify the category as a whole. But in reality this is not the way we think about categories in everyday speech. Typically we recognize that there are good examples and bad ones. A good example of a bird is a robin. An ostrich is also a bird, but it is a bad example. This creates considerable ambiguity in conversation. Everything is clear and simple when we use the word bird and are thinking of a robin. But when we speak of a bird and are actually thinking of an ostrich, there is plenty of room for confusion.

One might suppose that, given the way we use words in daily speech, this sort of problem would arise all the time, with continual confusion and misunderstanding. But most of the time this does not seem to happen. Somehow the problem of ambiguity is managed. Evidently conversation is not just about coding and decoding messages. It is this second aspect of conversation, revolving around ambiguity, that we are calling interpretation.

For the kind of product development activity that we think of as creative, this is a much better description of the sort of conversations that occur among designers and between designers and customers than the exchange of unambiguous, Morse-Code-like signals. And it leads us to focus on what is actually going on in those spaces in which interpretive conversations take place, and how such spaces are established to begin with.

How does a manager initiate these interpretive conversations and keep them going in the face of pressure to solve problems and bring closure? Here, the metaphor of the manager as hostess at a cocktail party provides a useful guide. At most cocktail parties, the guests are relative strangers. They are invited because they might have something interesting to say to one another, but only the hostess really knows what that is, and even she is not always sure. To make the party a success, she will often invite enough people so that it does not really matter if any one pair of them fails to hit it off.

Once the party is under way, her job is to keep the conversation flowing. A skilled hostess will introduce new people into groups where conversation seems to be flagging, or she will intervene to introduce a new topic when two people do not seem to be able to discover what they have in common on their own. She may break up groups that do not seem to be working or are headed for an unpleasant argument and steer the guests to other groups.

Like the chatter at any good cocktail party, the conversations about customer needs and technical possibilities in product development have a life of their own. At any given point it is not possible to say exactly where they are headed. And like cocktail party conversations, they are characterized by ambiguities and misunderstandings to begin with, especially when, as is usually the case with product development, they involve people of different backgrounds. At a cocktail party, where nothing of importance is at stake, people are prepared to work through these ambiguities until they arrive at a common understanding. And if they do not, it does not really matter. But in a business situation, where the stakes are high and there are potential conflicts of interest, the ambiguities can lead people to break off the conversation altogether. In such a situation, the skills of the hostess are at a premium.

The interpretive conversation is open-ended. If the conversations at a cocktail party were suddenly to come to an end, the party would be considered a failure. The highest compliment that can be paid to the hostess is that she has introduced people who will continue to see and interact with each other long after they have left the party.

The lessons of the cocktail party can be summarized in a series of distinct but closely related roles for the manager:

- Step One: choose the guests
- Step Two: initiate the conversation
- Step Three: keep the conversation going
- Step Four: refresh the conversation with new ideas

Choosing the Guests

For the manager, putting together a "guest list" presents a twofold problem: identifying people with the right background and selecting particular representatives who will engage in the conversation effectively. There is no exact formula for specifying the different backgrounds that should be present at the party, and obviously this will vary from one situation to another. But in our particular case studies, people seemed to err more on the side of exclusion than inclusion.

This happened, for example, at Chiron, where scorn for market-driven innovation led the company to underestimate the role of clinical knowledge in making a scientific discovery economically viable. Similarly, Levi's would have preferred to circumvent the whole conversational process by cross-training its designers in chemical engineering. And the very idea of the heavyweight manager is that you do not need a conversation with other people at all if the talking can take place inside one person's head. Picking the right interlocutors may mean selecting a lead customer who will be particularly exigent but also bring valuable knowledge to the table (Motorola's strategy). Aspect used operating room nurses as salespeople in order to screen potential users for those who would be strongly disposed toward using the equipment.

The interpretive manager must also balance the benefits of drawing different specialist communities and user groups into the conversation at the outset against the risk that, if too many people speaking too many different languages try to enter the conversation at the same time, the capacity for communication—still weak at that point—may be overloaded. This could lead to a breakdown in the conversation almost before it gets started.

Getting the Conversation Going

Once the guests have been selected, they must be encouraged to come to the party and to talk with one another. The difficulty of doing this depends, of course, on the institutional setting. At one extreme, within a single business organization the "guests" can be ordered to the party, although perhaps not forced to engage with one another once they get there. In other situations they may be drawn into the conversation by intellectual curiosity; this is typically the way collaborations begin at universities. In certain settings participation is driven by economic incentives. For example, companies generally feel compelled to participate in discussions of potential regulatory actions that may affect their business. Matsushita pulled out of the cellular infrastructure business partly because it felt excluded from full participation in the U.S. regulatory deliberations about the selection of technical standards for the industry, an episode to which we will return to in Chapter 6.

Those who convene the meeting may hold a key technological asset that motivates guests to join the conversation. Intel, as the architect of each new generation of microprocessors for personal computers, was able to attract firms developing computer peripherals in just this way. As we will see in more detail in Chapter 5, Intel sells its microprocessors to computer manufacturers, and the market for the chips depends on the market for the computers in which they are embedded. That market, in turn, depends on consumers' interest in the enhanced computing power offered by the new chips and their willingness to replace existing machines—or, less frequently nowadays, to buy a machine for the first time—in order to obtain that power. But consumer interest in computing power depends in part on the existence of attractive peripheral products that are compatible with Intel's chips and utilize their enhanced power. The peripherals and the chip must be developed in parallel in order to be ready for the market at the same time. In each case the designs are unknown in advance and emerge only gradually as development proceeds, but the chip and the peripherals must evolve in a way that yields compatibility in the end. Yet Intel has no direct control over the peripheral producers. Managing a conversation among these diverse but highly interested parties is one of Intel's major corporate challenges.[4]

In most economic environments, conversation is inhibited by fear of disclosing competitive assets and, not infrequently, a general climate of suspicion and mistrust. The central problem, then, becomes one of inducing the invitees to "open up." One approach is to offer free or discounted access to a product in exchange. Thus, Aspect provided its anesthesia monitoring equipment to highly respected anesthesiologists so that they could "play around" with it; in return, Aspect expected them to be forthcoming with their results. It did not do this indiscriminately, however: an effort was made to select physicians who would be interested in using the equipment in this way. Later, Aspect charged them for equipment use, although at a highly discounted price, with the presumption that clinicians who were not willing to participate in a conversation about the new technology would be screened out. Similarly, Chiron made its diagnostic assays freely available to laboratory researchers, again in the expectation that they would try them out in various ways and then discuss unusual outcomes with the company's scientists and technicians.

INNOVATION—THE MISSING DIMENSION

A similar tactic is a kind of gift exchange in which a company deliberately discloses critical technological information of possible commercial value in order to draw a potential participant into the conversation. Both the Italian jeans laundry Martelli and American Garment Finishers of El Paso mentioned doing this with other laundries in order to stimulate open technical discussions. Martelli also selectively revealed finishing ideas to its customers in an effort to overcome their reluctance to work with a firm that was also working with their competitors.

American Garment Finisher's president Claude Blankiet, who came to play a key role in the Levi's laundry network, traveled extensively to visit other laundries as well as washing-machine manufacturers and fabric and garment makers in order to exchange tricks of the trade. To illustrate the nature of these exchanges, he told a story about his first visit to a Japanese laundry that was having difficulty achieving a particular finishing effect. He volunteered the solution that he had used back home, and the proprietor, who had initially been distant and very reticent, then opened up and showed Blankiet several new processes his company had been working on. They talked freely about the merits of these processes and how to perfect them.

As this story shows, the interpretive manager often gets the conversation going by offering specific topics for discussion. The "technology shelf" at Motorola's cellular infrastructure group is a case in point. A small team of engineers was pulled together with the ostensible goal of reducing the volume required for a base station installation by a specified amount, and, more broadly, of anticipating new technologies that would be needed in future generations of the company's infrastructure products and to develop them ahead of time. Once identified and developed, the technologies would be "put on the shelf," ready when needed. From an analytical perspective, the purpose of the technology shelf was clear and focused. But from an interpretive perspective, its main function was to stimulate forward-looking conversations among the different communities and departments involved in new product development. The result was to strengthen the company's ability to move rapidly to introduce whatever innovative products its future situation might call for. From this perspective, the quantitative goal was less important than the quality of the conversations it stimulated.

Keeping the Conversation Going

In the early stages of a cocktail party, before the participants' common interests have been discovered, those who have been brought together may have great difficulty understanding one another at all. At this stage, when the means of communication are so primitive, it is difficult to distinguish genuine misunderstandings from deliberate distortions. There is a high likelihood of miscommunication and, where business issues are at stake, many possibilities for opportunistic behavior, which can easily lead to mistrust and a complete breakdown of the conversation. The highest priority of the interpretive manager at this early stage is to keep the discussion going—to carve out a space where the exchange of ideas is sheltered from the competitive pressures that might lead to breakdown. The university-like setting of Bell Labs provided such a space in the early days of cellular development at AT&T.

Later on, when the language of the new product is better developed and more broadly understood and the product itself is more mature, the interpretive role is somewhat different. At that point, although plenty of ambiguity may linger in the ongoing conversations among the developers and between developers and customers, and even though some of this misunderstanding may be opportunistically exploited, the risk of a complete communication breakdown is lower. A bigger concern at this stage is that the conversations will be overwhelmed by the imperatives of problem solving.

This was the prospect facing AT&T after it moved the cellular business out of Bell Labs into a separate business unit. In the course of the reorganization, all but two of the top fifteen managers from the Bell Labs era were replaced by career executives from the company's conventional lines of business. Of the two members of the original cellular team who were retained, one was assigned to an experimental manufacturing division with no product-line authority. With these moves, the institutional memory of the informal relationships cultivated in the early years of the business was erased.

The new cellular division was subject to the analytical procedures and hierarchy characteristic of the rest of the AT&T organization. In place of the informal interchange of the Bell Labs period, the company substituted a formal planning process. It also scheduled a limited number of day-long meetings with the other divisions of the company, which featured technical presentations along with some informal interaction. This exchange was necessary partly because the new organizational structure required the cellular division to rely on AT&T's telephone switching division for expertise in that area. The planning process and the meetings were drawn from a repertoire of procedures that had been designed to facilitate integration across the company as a whole. The new structure did in fact allow a flow of practical information among the various units. But with the dispersion of the original cellular team, the interpretive community that had grown up at Bell Labs—with its open-ended conversations and high tolerance for ambiguity and uncertainty—was lost. The discussions among the units were too short and infrequent to regenerate or enrich the language that had emerged in the original interpretive phase.

Refreshing the Conversation

The last phase of the interpretive process that is suggested by the cocktail party metaphor involves preventing the conversation from getting stale and perhaps petering out altogether through boredom and over-familiarity. Here the task of the interpretive manager is to keep refreshing the conversation and displacing its center of gravity. One way is to introduce new topics into the discussion.

An example is the "6-Sigma" quality program pioneered by Motorola during the 1980s and subsequently adopted by many other companies. Its purpose was to reduce to very low levels the probability of nonconformance to specifications. (The name of the program refers to the precision and repeatability with which a technical process is carried out. The goal implied by "6-Sigma," or six standard deviations from the mean performance, is a nonconformance probability of less than one in three hundred thousand.) As a senior executive at Motorola explained in an interview, "It doesn't really matter what the goal is exactly, as long as it is reasonable. The point is to stimulate, to catalyze." Motorola did not, in fact, reach its numerical target, but the 6-Sigma program precipitated many new and beneficial collaborations within the company, and later also with its suppliers, a large fraction of which were unanticipated at the outset.

Another way to refresh the conversation is to bring new people from different backgrounds into the group. The importance of changing the mix of people in the conversation is underscored by the case of Hewlett-Packard's alliance with Philips Medical Systems. HP had been successful in developing and marketing imaging systems in cardiology, and it wished to move into the radiological and vascular imaging markets. From HP's point of view, the chief asset that Philips brought to the table was the sales force it had developed in the radiology field for its x-ray and MRI equipment. But the interaction with Philips had a more fundamental impact. It radically altered HP's perception of the new market opportunity. HP learned from Philips that the barrier to a successful sales campaign was not the company's marketing concept but its technological concept. Cardiology equipment is designed to capture images of blood flows, whereas radiology equipment is designed to capture images of organs. For organ imaging, where a key objective is to find structural abnormalities, the quality sought was a high degree of resolution that would enable tissue differentiation. For cardiology imaging, the quality sought is accuracy in measuring flow velocity. Vascular imaging requires a combination of the two. The alliance between the two groups continued after Hewlett-Packard spun off its medical imaging group as part of Agilent Technologies, and soon afterward became closer still when Agilent sold all of its healthcare businesses, including the cardiology imaging unit, to Philips.

Disruptive Innovation

Each of these roles for the interpretive manager—identifying the "guests," bringing them to the table, initiating the conversation, keeping it going, and refreshing it from time to time—can also be viewed analytically, as problems to be solved. Managers therefore need to be clear about the analytical-interpretive distinction and about what they are trying to achieve. If they are not, there is a high likelihood that specific actions will fail to deliver the benefits that managers are seeking.

This point is illuminated by *The Innovator's Dilemma*, Clay Christensen's influential book on disruptive innovations and how to manage them.[5] The basic puzzle posed by the book is why so many successful, well-run companies find it so difficult to sustain their success over long periods. The explanation, according to Christensen, is that the same factors that are responsible for their success can and often do lead these companies to be blindsided by new technology that is simpler and cheaper than the incumbent product even though, at least initially, it cannot match performance. The leading companies in an industry almost invariably fail to recognize the significance of these "disruptive" innovations because their largest, most important clients have no interest in them to begin with. New competitors, with no ties to those customers and more incentive to serve the smaller, less profitable, or otherwise peripheral customers in the industry, are quicker to see the potential of the disruptive technologies and often end up riding them up the learning curve to industry dominance, dislodging the old leaders in the process. Well-known examples of such technologies include steel minimills, which have displaced traditional integrated steel mills in a growing number of market segments; minicomputers, which eventually displaced centralized mainframe computers; personal computers, which eventually displaced minicomputers; and so on.

According to Christensen, on the rare occasions when successful, industry-leading companies have actually become the disruptors rather than the disruptees, they have created autonomous units to commercialize the disruptive technology. These units, because of their organizational (and often physical) isolation from the rest of the firm and their relatively small size, have engaged with smaller, marginal customers that would have been dismissed as unprofitable distractions by the mainstream business units. Christensen cites the case of Hewlett-Packard's successful introduction of the inkjet printer. This product was, in performance terms, markedly inferior to the company's established and highly profitable laser printer product line, and it also yielded significantly lower profits. But its lower cost was attractive to a new population of customers—students and other individuals who depend on personal computers but cannot afford laser printers. To commercialize the inkjet printer, HP created a new business unit in Vancouver, Washington, that was completely independent from the established laser printer division in Boise, Idaho.[6] Christensen prescribes a similar strategy for other companies that are seeking to manage disruptive technologies.

Christensen's prescription is fundamentally analytical in character: the main function of the autonomous business unit is to *implement* the disruptive technology solution. But the same organizational approach can also be considered from an interpretive perspective, with very different implications. The differences are illustrated by Lutron's decision to create what it called the Cardinal unit. Cardinal was assigned the role of seeking out custom orders that could not be manufactured out of the company's standard lighting-control products. From an analytical perspective, Cardinal looked very much like Christensen's prescription. It was deliberately separated from the established business units and held, at least initially, to a different (and lesser) standard of profitability. One of the ideas was to give the fledgling unit some room to try its wings and to protect it from claims on the firm's marketing, capital, and other resources made by the powerful mainstream businesses.

But Cardinal was different from Christensen's prescription in one important respect. From the outset, Lutron's CEO, Joel Spira, conceived of Cardinal in interpretive terms. It was to be a locus for new conversations with customers who had special needs, and out of those talks new ideas for products would emerge. Spira's organizational vision for Cardinal as a separate organizational unit on the periphery of the main-stream market was consistent with that interpretive mission. Unless the conversation with these special customers was given its own table at the party, it would be drowned out by the ongoing dialog with Lutron's most important clients. As it turned out, after Cardinal departed from that original vision and started to behave in the analytical way prescribed by Christensen, it ran into problems. Cardinal's management tried to expand the unit's domain of operations and become an independent profit center. In selecting orders on the basis of profitability rather than innovative potential and competing with other parts of the company for orders that could, with minor modifications to their specifications, have been met out of standard components, the Cardinal unit corrupted its original, interpretive mission, and at that point it was dismantled.

Disruptive innovations pose a threat whenever a successful firm cuts itself off from customers on the periphery of the market who are an important source of insight into technological possibilities. Managers can address this problem from either an analytical or an interpretive perspective. In the former case, the best advice might be to organize a systematic process for gathering information about technology trends from a wide range of sources, including different groups of customers; then, to apply a set of objective criteria to determine which of the new technologies are likely to be disruptive; and then, to establish an autonomous business unit to implement the disruptive technology. This is essentially Christensen's recommended approach.

From the interpretive perspective, the most important advice would be to identify the most interesting customers on the periphery, find a way to bring them to the table, and engage them in open-ended conversation over an extended period. Creating a separate organization for this purpose may or may not be the best approach; there are advantages in either case. But the central point is that the organizational choices will be different depending on whether it is the interpretive or the analytical perspective that is being adopted. If managers are unaware of the analytical–interpretive distinction, their range of choice will be narrower than it should be.

Language and Ambiguity

The danger of the drive to clarify is that it often reifies insight, to the point of eliminating the very conditions of uncertainty that are needed for creativity to flourish. The analytical approach typically assumes that the ambiguities have already been eliminated, or, if they still remain, the basic thrust is to get rid of them.

But just as a cocktail party would be tedious in the extreme if all the guests had the same background and agreed about every idea, a business organization from which ambiguity has been removed is unlikely to produce anything very innovative and interesting. In product development as in cocktail parties, the ambiguities make the give and take of discussions worthwhile. By purging their organizations of open-ended conversation, ambiguity, and interpretation, product development managers diminish their sense of what is possible.

Anyone who has ever attended a real cocktail party knows that what makes these events interesting initially is that they bring together people from different walks of life. When people do not know one another to begin with, sometimes that lack of knowledge and understanding is what makes the party sparkle. As people try to explore their differences, they are drawn deeper into conversations. But at other times a lack of understanding can ruin the party. People become irritated or even angry with one another and walk away from the conversational group. Sometimes they leave the party altogether. Anticipating these different reactions and figuring out ways to keep the conversation going are critical parts of the hostess's role.

They are also critical parts of the manager's role in the early stages of product development. But why does what is ostensibly the same situation elicit such divergent reactions? Why do people sometimes break off the conversation and on other occasions keep talking? The key to this question lies in the difference between ambiguity and misunderstanding. One way to gain insight into that difference is to think about how *language communities* emerge. We argue that the development and introduction of new products is like the development of new language communities.

There is certainly a literal sense in which this is true. As any marketer will attest, new products gain traction in the marketplace when people start talking about them, and the best traction comes when people start talking about radically new products in radically new ways (chat rooms, texting, hybrid cars). In this sense, the emergence of new language may be a necessary condition for innovation. But the analogy also works at a more fundamental level. The participants in conversations that may lead to new products typically are drawn from different language communities, in the sense that they have different specialties and think and talk differently from each other. In the early stages of product development, they do not yet have a common language. How does that language develop?

Language scholars have studied the development of new languages in a variety of situations, including trading communities, where strangers from different language groups and radically distinct cultures come into contact with one another, and groups of deaf people, who are brought together without any common system of communication. The emergence of new language in these situations follows a systematic pattern. The first generation of language is a pidgin, a stripped-down traders' language without a developed grammar. The children who grow up playing with one another in these hybrid communities develop a second-generation language, called a creole. It incorporates the pidgin vocabulary but adds to it a fully developed grammar. Although the creole may not be formally recognized or written down, it is a real language in that it has the formal properties that linguistic scholars recognize in more fully established languages. But for our purposes the most interesting difference between a pidgin and a creole is that in a pidgin communications are clear and unambiguous. It is in the more developed and sophisticated outgrowth of the pidgin, the creole, that ambiguity starts to play a role. Thus, language evolves from clarity to ambiguity—precisely the opposite direction of evolution that one finds in analytical problem solving. Language development evolves, in other words, *toward the creation of interpretive space.*

Something similar happens when people try to learn a second language as adults. At the beginning, the new language is a total confusion; it sounds like a babble. If, in the face of the babble, you do not abandon the effort and continue to listen, you begin to realize that at certain moments you actually do understand what people are saying. As time goes on, the number of those moments increases. But in these early stages of learning, your understanding seems to be binary: you either get it or you don't. Either way, you have no idea why. If you don't understand, the best you can do is to ask the speaker to repeat what she is saying more slowly and hope that it will come across the second time around. But it is too embarrassing to keep asking for repetition all the time. And since you cannot pinpoint the source of the confusion when you are not understanding, even when you think you do understand you are not sure whether you really do.

The real breakthrough in learning a new language comes when you can actually identify the source of your problem, when you can specify what exactly is blocking your comprehension. At that point, you can in principle ask for specific clarification (although of course you may still be too embarrassed to do so). Sometimes the source of the problem is a particular word or phrase that you have never encountered before. But frequently your difficulty centers on the interpretation of an expression that is genuinely ambiguous even to the native speaker.

This final problem in our understanding of language never disappears. When it becomes the central problem, we have reached the third stage in language acquisition. At this stage we can unfailingly separate out problems of interpretation from ignorance of a particular phrase. It is a stage that always eludes some non-native speakers. But the direction of evolution is clear. Once again, as with the development of a new language, the evolution is toward the creation of a space for interpretation.

These insights into language add weight to the metaphor of product development as a cocktail party. They suggest that the conversations between designers and their clients, as well as the conversations among different kinds of designers, involve three distinct processes. One, like the development of a new language, moves systematically toward ambiguity from a starting point of clear, very simple communication. The second, analogous to the drawing of new members into an existing language community, also moves toward ambiguity, but from a starting point of total confusion. In both processes there is a stage at which people cannot be sure whether the communication problems they are experiencing are caused by confusion and misunderstanding or by genuine differences of interpretation. A complete breakdown of communication can easily happen at this stage, especially in business situations where opportunistic behavior—one side seeking to gain at the other's expense—is always a threat. But if the participants keep talking, they will eventually begin to participate in the third kind of process—a conversation among members of an established language community, in which ambiguity can be clearly recognized for what it is, and for the richness that it brings to the exchange of ideas.

Thinking about product development and innovation in terms of the development of new language communities thus fleshes out the cocktail party metaphor. It helps us to understand what might cause the conversation to break up, and it also reveals more clearly what is at stake if the party is not a success.

THE MISSED CONNECTIONS OF
MODERN MANAGEMENT

4

Some of the most impressive managers we met in the course of our research could look at the world simultaneously through both analytical and interpretive lenses and flip back and forth between them as conditions required. Lutron's Joel Spira is one of those managers who understands, instinctively, the two approaches. As the company's founder, Spira has dominated Lutron and has been able to pick his role in this privately held company. In recent years he has focused mainly on the interpretive aspects of new product development because that is what interests him most, and he has built a management team to complement him whose strengths are analytical. But Spira has also frequently inserted himself into problem-solving projects.

Most of the managers we encountered did not have this ability. For the majority, the pull of the analytical approach was so powerful and its routines so ingrained into management practice that they could not imagine taking a different tack. Challenges that might more usefully have been treated as open-ended, where multiple possibilities could coexist and play off one another, were therefore forced back into the problem-solving mode, where the emphasis was on clarifying the task, getting things straight, eliminating the redundant, the ambiguous, the unknown. Moreover, even those who did seem to have an intuitive grasp of the two approaches could not clearly articulate where and when they would favor one over the other, or why.

This came as a surprise to us. Over the past two decades, a host of new concepts, tools, and maxims has entered the managerial lexicon, each of them intended to help firms respond to a business environment that seems to have become increasingly unpredictable. Process specialists emphasize quality management, learning organizations, and team leadership skills. Technology vendors offer IT infrastructure and enterprise management applications that promise vastly more efficient communication up and down the supply chain. Business theorists and consultants preach the virtues of matrix management methods, network structures, virtual corporations, and flat, decentralized, boundaryless organizations. A central purpose of all these approaches—we refer to them collectively as the *new management*—is to increase the flexibility of the firm and to accelerate the speed with which it can adapt to rapid and unforeseen changes in its environment. Each sees more effective organizational integration as the key to greater flexibility. Each is concerned with how to combine the efforts of different individuals or departments quickly and efficiently, and how to work effectively across the firm's boundaries with its suppliers, its customers, and in some cases its rivals.

But our field research revealed a kind of disconnect between this surge of managerial advice and what was actually happening on the ground in the firms we were studying.

Most of the design and product development managers we interviewed hardly referred to these concepts at all. What could explain this short-circuit between the management literature and the people we interviewed?

Perhaps the new ideas had been absorbed so thoroughly that they had become part of the managerial furniture—taken for granted and for that reason not thought to be worth discussing. Or perhaps they were not mentioned because they did not seem relevant to the problems at hand. We came to believe that both explanations were true. Many of the tools and concepts of the new management did seem to have become second-nature to our interviewees, and for certain purposes they were clearly extremely effective. But in other situations, they did not seem to help at all; they seemed one-dimensional and even clichéd. Two of them—"Listen to the voice of the customer" and "Focus on your core competencies"—illustrate this problem particularly well. Not coincidentally, these are two of the most prominent aphorisms of the new management literature.

The Voice of the Customer

In the analytical view, the customer has preexisting needs, and the job of the developer is to identify those needs and then to create products that meet them in an optimal way. This is seen as the basic purpose of product development projects, and a battery of sophisticated techniques such as Quality Function Deployment is available to enhance the precision and fidelity with which the customer's needs are captured.[1]

In the interpretive view, the customer has no needs until they are articulated, and this articulation is what the interaction between designer and customer is all about. The prototype of this kind of interaction takes place between an architect and her client. The client begins by talking about the building he thinks he would like. His ideas at this early stage are typically quite vague. The architect then sketches two or three rough drawings. The client looks at the sketches and points out where they seem inadequate, using them to try to explain to the architect what he now has in mind, but also rethinking what he wants in light of the architect's interpretations. In the course of the conversation, the architect may ask why one or another feature of the client's proposal is desirable and suggest an alternative way of achieving that aim. During this process, the client may realize that two of the three drawings have features that should be incorporated into the final design. The architect then produces another sketch that reflects this conversation with her client but is also influenced, perhaps, by another building she has recently observed or by a colleague's critique. The client looks at the new drawing and tries to restate (and rethink) what he really wants. And so it goes through the schematic design phase, until client and architect arrive at a common general understanding of the building.

The schematic design process is iterative, but not in the way that engineers use an iterative strategy to arrive at the optimal solution to a predefined problem. That approach would lead one to think that the client comes to the architect with a specific end in mind and with a set idea of the resources he is prepared to put into the project. The architect would, as necessary, lead the client to compromise that initial vision in light of technical constraints that she as an expert brings to bear on the project and would then produce increasingly faithful renderings of the modified vision.

But what actually happens in such interactions is usually quite different. During the back and forth between architect and client, the client's original ideas about what he wants change substantially, and the architect's ideas about how to give form to these ideas will also undergo modification. Out of this conversational process, something new is created, something that neither architect nor client imagined before it began. What is taking place here is a process of mutual discovery. It is not problem solving in the conventional sense. This basic insight—that architect and client are engaged in a process of joint discovery—is transferable to the product development domain, even though no single customer may exist with whom the designer can converse.

But that is not how the injunction to "listen to the voice of the customer" is commonly understood today. What is "new" in this new management aphorism that was missing from the old management prescriptions are techniques for precisely identifying the customer's desires. This shift reflects the decline of the mass-production system, in which economies of scale in the production of a single standardized product so dramatically reduced costs that customers could be induced to buy a standard product no matter how remote it was from their specific needs. Recent advances in information technology, along with associated gains in flexible manufacturing techniques, have greatly reduced the cost of product variety. Innovations in information technology have also made it possible to identify different customers' preferences for specific product features more precisely, more quickly, and more cost-effectively and to market products to these groups and subgroups directly.

But while the new technologies of production may have made it less costly to accommodate customers' particular preferences, this is not the same thing as saying that the customer actually knows what those preferences are. Designs are social objects and depend for their meaning on the context in which they are used. A designed object does not exist in isolation but only in relation to other objects that surround and complement it and signal its use. Sometimes that meaning may be evident to everybody and well understood and articulated. Think, for example, of the interior decorators' urge to push the faceplate of a dimmer switch back so that it is flush to the wall. But in many cases the designer's problem, like the architect's, is to enter into the customer's world and understand and interpret the context in which the object is used.

No obvious formula exists for working one's way into an initially alien world, but in our case studies the firms that came closest were the garment firms. They actually made a deliberate and concerted effort to enter into their customers' world (or worlds). Levi's broke its youth market into age segments and assigned a designer to follow each segment, visiting the clubs that his age group frequented, shopping in stores where they shopped, eavesdropping on conversations of kids as they looked at records or picked through the racks of used jeans. The different designers then met to discuss what they had observed and what this implied about the direction in which the company should move. A number of firms in different industries opened their own retail outlets where they could continuously watch their customers shop.

In trying to interpret the customer's world, the designer must look at two different and contradictory dimensions of the design. One is the way in which a design object enters, or could enter, that world *in use*. In this respect the designer wants to make the object ready-at-hand, transparent but not completely invisible, present and available for the customer to reach for automatically when he or she needs it, without thinking. The other is the object as *style*, a sign or a signal of where the customer stands in a social universe. For this the object needs to have high visibility. But just as the sound of a word usually has nothing to do with its meaning, the signaling value of an object is generally independent of its function in use. The signal, moreover, is complex; it must indicate to outsiders the user's membership in a group, but it must also express her individuality to others within the group.

One might expect that in their conversations designers would attempt to separate out these different dimensions. In jeans, for example, the evolution of design is being driven in part by the attempt to reproduce the comfort of a used garment, softening the fabric by washing it in various ways. This effort is in principle distinct from changes in the silhouette, like baggy jeans or bell bottoms, which are fashion items. But in practice the distinction is difficult to maintain. The look and feel of the jeans becomes a style factor and extends to the silhouette of the wallet on the back pocket and the moustache of creases in the crotch.

The chief designer for Nokia described a moment when his company connected viscerally with the critical importance of style in cell phones.[2] A group of Nokia engineers who were drinking after work in a Helsinki bar each put their phones on the table. When one of the phones rang, every engineer reached to answer it, but because the phones and their rings were identical, there was great confusion about which phone belonged to whom and whose phone had actually rung. Individualization in the look and sound of cell phones eventually made it possible for engineers and everyone else to reach for their own phone automatically, without giving it much thought. But it also provided an opportunity for style to enter the cellular world so that the look distinguishes the person as an individual. As Nokia's head designer sat with his interviewer in a Helsinki café, he could read the background and personality of people walking down the street from the phones they were carrying. This kind of sensitivity in a design team does not come from simply assuming that the customer has a voice and the designer's job is merely to listen to it.

Even when the designer can talk to the customer directly, how much does the customer's voice really help? It is not obvious that the customer's voice is any more important than the designer's in imagining new products. Patrick le Quément, the chief designer at Renault, tells a story that is germane to this point. Partly in reaction to the blandness of the "world car" concept, le Quément pursued designs that expressed the particular national context in which a car was built. He did this first at Volkswagen in Germany, and when he moved to Renault, he sought to reorient that company's designs to reflect the character of his native France. But the design team he put together for this purpose was 40 percent foreign. When asked to explain the rationale for this choice, he told the story of the fisherman standing on the bank of the river who asked the fish, "How is the water?" To which the fish replied, "What water?"

The company and its products are themselves part of the consumer's world—a world which the company tries both to understand and to create. The story of how Levi's designed a line of baggy jeans makes clear how blurry the line is between these two activities. Levi's had spotted the baggy jeans style as it was emerging from the youth culture of the inner city, where it had become a hallmark of rappers. (Presumably baggy pants made it easier to hide guns and other contraband.) The company concluded early on that the fashion trend would spread to the general culture as hip-hop music itself grew in popularity, and it invested heavily in designs rooted in this trend.

But demand for these jeans began to level off much sooner than Levi's expected. At that point, the company launched an intensive advertising campaign featuring its new jeans in hip-hop settings. The campaign succeeded in generating a second, larger wave of demand for the new fashion, particularly among suburban teenagers. But our respondents in the interviews confessed that they did not know whether they had revived an existing trend or had created a new one; and it was unclear to them whether it was the baggy jeans, the hip-hop music, or the advertisements themselves to which customers were reacting. In a similar story, an Italian jeans company built an advertising campaign around a fictional Polish rock star and was then forced, under pressure, to find a person who would play in real life the character it had portrayed in its ad campaign.

This interplay is not limited to fashion. It is equally true of useful objects. Thus, the infrared remote control device that Lutron developed to turn off the light switch from across the room depended on the customer's earlier experience with remote controls for televisions and garage doors. The consumer was "led" to understand the device by the evolution of the environment in which he lived.

Sometimes, companies themselves can lead that evolution. Consider the design team at Chrysler that was charged with developing a next-generation minivan. As Kamal Malek has shown, the challenge confronting the Chrysler team was formidable: how to come up with a product that would allow the company to maintain its dominant position in the minivan segment at a time when more and more competitors were entering that market. Chrysler had practically invented the modern minivan, and over the years it had become the company's most visible mainstream product and also one of its most profitable. Achieving continued leadership not only required the development team to correctly identify and preserve those aspects of the original vehicle that had made it such a success but also to find new features that would cause the new model to stand out.[3]

The Chrysler team responded to these challenges in two radically different ways. On the one hand, it put unusually heavy emphasis on a strategy of listening to the voice of the customer, making the systematic collection, analysis, and prioritization of highly detailed customer input an integral part of the design process. On the other hand, it also relied on an approach that team members described variously as "following their gut feel" and "a nontraditional kind of decision-making"—an approach that seemed to contradict the voice of the customer and that we came to understand as essentially interpretive in character.

One result of this process which turned out to be very important to the eventual success of the new minivan was the addition of a second sliding door on the left side of the vehicle, the so-called fourth door, which neither Chrysler nor its competitors had offered until then. The case for the fourth door was not indicated by market research—indeed, the initial reaction of potential customers to the idea was often strongly negative on safety grounds. ("That's the traffic side! We don't want our kids jumping out!")

Despite this, the design team persisted with the fourth door, believing in this case that they knew more about their customers' requirements than did the customers themselves. In effect they were saying to their customers, "You don't really know what features you need on this vehicle; just tell us what you want to do with it, how you want to use it, and we'll tell you what you need." Their confidence stemmed from their thorough understanding of the background, concerns, and interests of users. Many members of the design team were themselves living the life of the typical minivan user (the team included some soccer moms), and they knew how often they had been inconvenienced by the current configuration. It was this rich contextual understanding that led the designers to interpret what the customers were saying as a need (of which the customers themselves were unaware) for the fourth door.

The decision turned out to be a good one. Not only were 85 percent of the new Chrysler minivans ordered with that option, but Chrysler's competitors were forced to scramble to respond, initially by offering rebates on their existing minivans and later by redesigning (at great expense) their next season's lineup to offer the same option. Chrysler's decision to go with a fourth door was credited with changing the dynamics of the entire minivan market segment.

Core Competencies

A second major prescription of the new management literature is that a firm should limit its activities to its core competencies. Compared with listening to the voice of the customer, it is a little less clear what this prescription is reacting against. In part, it is the notion of the old, tightly integrated corporation, of which the canonical example is Ford Motor Company's original River Rouge Plant, where iron and coal came in one end and the finished car came out the other. The company's activities extended forward even further to car dealerships and financing and backward toward its own coal and iron mines. But the adage can also be read as a reminder of the dangers of conglomeration, with firms seeking to grow by acquiring collections of unrelated businesses and, as happened to many conglomerates in the 1970s and 80s, finding themselves poorly equipped to manage them. Read as a warning against a company's trying to do too much, there is little in our case material that would call this aphorism into question.

But as a positive guide to what the company *should* do, the advice is highly misleading. The problem lies in its implication that the economy can be deconstructed into a set of basic elements—the competencies—and that certain of these will be key to the firm's competitive position. But in fact it is precisely the dissolution of the sharp boundaries between the different components of the economic structure that is the hallmark of the new economy. Thus, if River Rouge is emblematic of the old economy, the integration of the computing, office equipment, imaging, photography, and communication industries which brought Kodak, IBM, Xerox, Motorola, and AT&T into direct competition with one another is emblematic of the new. Product development in all of our cases involved not winnowing and focusing on a particular set of competencies but, on the contrary, integrating across competencies that used to be distinct: radio and telephone in the cellular case; basic science and clinical practice in medical devices; textiles, garments, and laundries in the fashion jeans industry.

In the analytical view, the firm identifies a set of core competencies that it then may or may not decide to embrace as its own. What the interpretive approach suggests, however, is that the question for the firm is how to introduce itself into the kinds of intense interactions (that is, conversations) that will lever the competencies it brings from its past activities.

The analytical view of core competencies, with its notion of closed, well-defined borders, also infects two other terms widely used in the new management literature: networks and teams. Networks are generally contrasted with the traditional hierarchical, bureaucratic organization. They are often presented as a set of nodes connected to one another by crisscrossing channels of communication. But there are two different ways of understanding the relationships among the nodes and the channels of communication between them. One view treats the nodes as self-contained units or islands, very much as if they were the organizational counterparts of competencies, and looks for other institutions and organizations to form the links between them. When there is no link, this literature sees a "structural hole" and hence opportunities for improvement (and in a market system, profit) through arbitrage.[4] But an alternative view is that the nodes must be linked by conversations that eventually break down the isolation of the islands.

Similarly, there are two different ways of understanding teams. The dominant perspective is the analytical one: teams are composed of different members who bring particular competencies to the group, and the teams can form or reform depending on what competencies are required. But an alternative view is that teams can be organic groups that develop their own language and understanding over time and become something greater than merely the sum of their competencies.

These different views of competencies, networks, and teams can be seen in each of our three industry cases. In the cellular case, the difference is most evident in the problem all the companies faced concerning what to do about the switch. The switch connects the cellular system to the landline telephone networks and also handles complicated allocation and billing functions for the system as a whole. Three of the five companies we visited—AT&T, Nokia, and Eriksson—produced their own switches for landline systems before they began cellular development. Two—Motorola and Matsushita—did not. It is difficult to imagine a meaningful list of core competencies for a cellular company that would not include switching technology.

Matsushita exited the infrastructure segment of the cellular business largely because it did not have this technology itself and was not prepared to invest in it. But the three companies that did have internal competencies in switching technology handled them very differently. Nokia in essence transferred the technological capability in switching to its cellular division; the new division was allowed to design and build its own switch, albeit starting from designs that had been passed to it from the landline switching division. Switching thus became an integral part of the ongoing cellular conversation at Nokia.

When AT&T's cellular effort was housed in Bell Labs, it also designed its own switches. But once cellular became a separate business unit, it was obliged to incorporate switches designed and built by the landline switching division, a totally separate organizational unit. At Ericsson, the cellular business unit used switches from the landline business unit from the outset, and this has continued. Both Ericsson and AT&T tried to compensate for the organizational (and geographic) distance between the switching and other cellular components by designating liaisons and scheduling formal meetings on a regular basis. But there was no ongoing, continuous interaction. The switch might as well have been purchased from an outside vendor.

Motorola actually did purchase its switches on the outside. But in its search for a solution to the switch problem, it sought much closer collaboration between the switch and the rest of the cellular infrastructure than either AT&T or Ericsson, and it initially considered developing a switch internally. After rejecting this alternative, it sought a strategic alliance with a non-U.S. producer, but that alliance ultimately failed, reportedly because of a cultural difference: the compensation and career incentives at Motorola were oriented toward long-term employment and benefits, whereas the corresponding structures at the partner company led their engineers to adopt much shorter time horizons. Differences in the legal environments in the two countries also made collaboration difficult. This example suggests the difficulties of bridging the cultural divide between organizations. But the examples of AT&T and Ericsson make clear that it is not enough to have all the competencies together under one roof either. In both cases, it is the boundaries that are critical.

The Deep Roots of Analysis

At the beginning of this chapter we stated that many of the prescriptions of the new management literature appeared one-dimensional and clichéd. We can now see why. The reason that prescriptions like "Listen to the voice of the customer" and "Focus on your core competencies" seem one-dimensional is because they really *are* one-dimensional. They are understood exclusively in analytical terms. The possibility of an interpretive reading is completely absent.

It is easy enough to criticize the superficiality and faddishness of much of the contemporary management literature. But such a diagnosis would be too easy in this case. The analytical bias has much deeper roots. It can be traced back as far as Adam Smith's great treatise *Wealth of Nations*, which was built around two essential ideas. One is that economic growth and development depend on the progressive division of labor into a set of separate operations and on the specialization of productive resources to perform these operations. The canonical example of this process is Smith's famous pin factory, where the master pinmaker who makes the whole pin is replaced by one worker who pulls the wire, a second worker who cuts the wire, a third who heads the pin, a fourth who points the pin, and so on. The second idea is that this process of specialization creates a problem of coordinating the specialized resources. In Smith, and in most of economic theory, that problem is solved by the prices generated in a competitive market. Later scholars came to recognize the bureaucratic corporation as an alternative solution in situations when the market is too narrow to permit competition. The formal rules and procedures of the corporate bureaucracy substitute for the price signals of the market as the means—the language—of coordination.

But each of these solutions to the coordination problem presents the same difficulty. Both languages—the language of prices and the language of corporate bureaucracies—are impoverished and stripped-down. They are impoverished because they are too complete. They preclude the very ambiguity that is the fulcrum for interpretation and the source of creativity. They are, in effect, pidgins. The difference between a pidgin and a true language is the ability of the latter to tolerate and handle ambiguity. And when economic activity is characterized by ambiguity, other organizational forms are required.

The new management literature can be understood as a response to this need. In today's volatile, unpredictable economic environment, in which ambiguity is pervasive and innovation is frequently about creating things that are unimaginable before they emerge, management experts advocate more flexible forms of organization—forms such as learning corporations, network structures, and cross-functional teams—in which the individual pieces relate to one another in a more complex way than is possible either through the price mechanism or in a classical corporate hierarchy. But without a vocabulary for the interpretive process, these prescriptions too easily slide back into the analytical mode.

There is, of course, a literature on the "softer" side of management that is closely related to our notion of interpretation.

It is fairly standard in this literature to make a distinction between two levels of knowledge and understanding. Thus, Douglas North distinguishes between *formal* and *informal* rules and institutions. Formal rules are the target of purposeful, self-interested behavior on the part of economic actors who seek to mold these rules in their favor. Informal rules are beyond the reach of the actors. Often implicit and unarticulated, they evolve independently of human volition.[5]

North's notion of informal rules recalls what Michael Polanyi termed *tacit knowledge,* a concept which has given rise to a substantial literature in the social sciences.[6] Tacit knowledge can be likened to the way we understand and use the grammatical rules of a language, an analogy that brings tacit knowledge very close to our own characterization of interpretation.[7]

The great economist Alfred Marshall in many ways anticipated Polanyi when he talked of the industrial districts of nineteenth-century Europe as territories where the inhabitants imbibed the knowledge that undergirded local industry along with the air they breathed. This notion has been revived in the recent literature on the Italian industrial districts and in high-tech districts like Silicon Valley in California.[8]

Donald Schön wrote about communities of practice— professional and craft communities bound together by a form of tacit knowledge very close to our notion of interpretation.[9] And the Japanese business scholars Ikujiro Nonaka and Hiro Takeuchi talk about the "knowledge-creating" company as playing upon the relationship between tacit and explicit knowledge. New knowledge, they argue, emerges in a cycling back and forth between practice, which is tacit, and the explicit interpretation of practice. For them, as for us here, the problem is the inability to conceptualize this kind of process. They argue that this is a defect of the Western, as opposed to the Asian, philosophical tradition.[10] Yet one can also find an opening for this way of thinking about business in the Western management literature.[11]

The difficulty with this formidable body of writing is that virtually all of the insights that might point to the interpretive side of management have also been presented, sometimes even by the same authors, in analytical terms. Take, for example, the network organization—a system of nodes connected by channels of communication. The sociologist Ronald Burt focuses on "structural holes" in these networks—nodes between which there is no communication.[12] And while connecting these nodes might be expected to entail the development of a common language and vocabulary, Burt thinks of it in terms of arbitrage, in which agents are attracted to the possibility of carrying information from one node to another, just as traders in a currency market might take advantage of the differential between the exchange rate in New York and London.

Similarly, we might think of the term *integration* as applying to the process through which an organization creates a new interpretive community, as occurred in the development of cell phones or fashion jeans. But that term has long been associated in the management literature with Lawrence and Lorsch, who use it essentially as a synonym for coordination.[13] Their notion of a necessary trade-off between integration and specialization actually encourages this reading. Yet there was no alternative to the integration of the radio and telephone specialties in the process through which the cell phone emerged; the preservation of the separate specialties in that case would have prevented the new product from emerging at all.

In the management section of many bookstores, *The Knowledge-Creating Company* by Nonaka and Takeuchi is displayed alongside Peter Senge's *The Fifth Discipline.*[14] Senge's book is also a critique of management practice. But the argument is basically that we are using the wrong analytical models. Our models are too linear and too simplistic, says Senge. He wants us to think instead about systems with intricate feedback loops. Such systems are too complex to be solved; they need instead to be simulated. It is a kind of "bounded rationality" critique. His is an argument not against analysis but in favor of a new, more profound analytical approach.

But the shorthand terms Senge uses are very close to those of Nonaka and Takeuchi. A "learning organization" sounds a lot like a "knowledge-creating company." Unless one reads very closely—much more closely than most people have time for—it is hard to see that they are really arguing for fundamentally different things. And precisely because Senge's message is so much more in keeping with our received ways of thinking, it tends to dominate. Indeed, Nonaka and Takeuchi end by reinforcing Senge's analytical way of looking at the world, instead of helping us to formulate a fundamentally different alternative.

The preeminent scholar of the relationship between the organizational structure of the firm and its decision-making capacity is the psychologist Karl Weick. The scope of his concerns is indicated by the phrase "sense-making," which appears in the titles of several of his works.[15] But from the point of view of the analytical–interpretive distinction, Weick identifies a long, undifferentiated list of problems that people face in "making sense" out of the world in which they operate. Most of those problems are created by a lack of the sort of information that the classic analytical models generally assume the decisionmaker has or can easily generate. They fall under the headings of information uncertainty and bounded rationality. Once again, insights that might contribute to an understanding of interpretation are quickly assimilated into analytical categories. Thus, for example, Weick introduces the notion of improvisation or "bricolage," in which practitioners from different engineering and craft disciplines work together in a kind of ad hoc way that avoids the contradictions and conflicts dividing the disciplines at an abstract or theoretical level.[16] Here again the collaboration between the telephone and radio engineers in the early cellular industry comes immediately to mind. But Weick's concept of improvisation could also be an approach in which the theoretical issues involved in this collaboration were not well understood or could not be resolved. In that case, it would be an example of bounded rationality—analysis in the face of a degree of uncertainty and complexity that formal decision-making tools and theory are unable to capture. For managers steeped in the analytical tradition, the notion of improvisation may enrich their vocabulary, but it does not help them to see that interpretation is a fundamentally different process.

For us, the most telling example of how the analytical perspective eclipses the interpretive is the way people perceive the Bauhaus school of design. The Bauhaus, which emerged in Weimar Germany in the 1920s, was perhaps the most influential school of design in the twentieth century. The school's design philosophy has come to be captured in the short-hand phrase "Form follows function," implying that the optimum or best design can be deduced directly from the function it is supposed to serve. In other words, the optimum design will be the one that solves the problem of how to perform that function most effectively. This concept is the antithesis of the notion of interpretation that we are developing here. And it was belied at the very beginning of our field work by the designs we encountered at Lutron: for example, the light dimmer in the form of a wand resembling a TV remote control, which worked as a design not because it solved the problem most effectively but because of the context of everyday life that had already grown up around the TV; or the click that the company built into its wall-mounted light dimmer to signal that the dimmer was turned off, even though the reduction in power was continuous and the click actually had no functional role to play at all.

It turns out that the phrase "Form follows function" did not come from the Bauhaus School at all but was coined much earlier by the nineteenth-century American architect Richard Sullivan.[17] What the Bauhaus designers actually advocated was that design should grow out of the integration of technology, craftsmanship, and art. And to achieve this end, they built a community of practitioners drawn from all three disciplines, whom they encouraged to participate in a set of continuing conversations, very much along the lines of the interpretive communities that grew up around cellular telephones, fashion jeans, and several medical devices we examined in our case studies.[18] But this is not the legacy of the Bauhaus that most people "remember." Here, even in our collective cultural memory, the analytical has trumped the interpretive.

Ambiguity without Paralysis

Organizations need closure, otherwise nothing can be accomplished. And there are many tools and techniques to help them achieve it. What managers lack is a framework that simultaneously allows them to keep things moving forward *without* closure. This is the value of the interpretive approach, and a basic thrust of this book is to make the interpretive approach more prominent and its implications clearer in the minds of today's managers. That is only the first step, however. The next and more difficult task is to see how the inter-

INNOVATION—THE MISSING DIMENSION

pretive and analytical approaches can be combined within the same organization without obscuring the fundamental differences between the two.

Most businesses need both approaches. They need to get new products into the market in a timely manner even as conversations with the customer and among the product development team continue. Conversely, they need to keep the general conversation going even as they are drawing particular new designs out of it and implementing the projects required to bring them to market. At different times or in different parts of the organization one of these perspectives may be more important than the other. Yet even those practitioners we interviewed who seemed intuitively to grasp both approaches could not clearly articulate where and when they would favor one over the other, or why.

In the next chapter we will describe some of the ways in which the analytical and interpretive approaches can be used together.

COMBINING ANALYSIS AND
INTERPRETATION

5

Most of the managers we interviewed during our research had difficulty talking about the interpretive processes in which they were engaged, and in the preceding chapters we have focused on developing a conceptual vocabulary for these processes and how to manage them. But the thrust of our argument is not to replace analytical with interpretive management. Innovative firms need both. Part of the problem in combining the two is that the interpretive approach is not fully recognized or well understood. But the problem goes beyond recognition and understanding. Ultimately, the inability of business practitioners to describe the activity that we are calling interpretation is a symptom of something deeper. Managing interpretive processes involves a way of thinking about the world that not only is very different from the analytical perspective but, at least along certain dimensions, is fundamentally at odds with it.

Analytical managers seek clarity and closure. They organize work into projects, with a well-defined beginning and end. Interpretation, by contrast, is an ongoing process, with no natural endpoint. Interpretive managers seek not to eliminate ambiguity but rather to work with and through it, using it as a resource out of which new discoveries and insights emerge. Analytical managers convene meetings to set goals and solve problems; interpretive managers invite conversations and set directions. In problem-solving projects, communication consists of the exchange of well-defined chunks of information; communication in interpretive processes is open-ended and context-dependent. In analysis, integration involves the coordination of specialists and the efficient assembling of the problem's component parts; in the interpretive view, integration entails the merging of horizons and the creation of new language. Iteration as an analytical strategy is employed by managers and engineers to converge on the optimal solution to a predefined problem; iteration as an interpretive strategy encourages interplay between designer and consumer which leads to something new that neither could have anticipated at the outset.

The main differences between the analytical and interpretive ways of looking at product development are summarized in the following chart.

ANALYSIS	INTERPRETATION
The focus is a project, with a well-defined beginning and end	The focus is a process, which is ongoing and open-ended
The thrust is to solve problems	The thrust is to discover new meanings
Managers set goals	Managers set directions

ANALYSIS	INTERPRETATION
Managers convene meetings and negotiate to resolve different viewpoints and eliminate ambiguity	Managers invite conversations and translate to encourage different viewpoints and explore ambiguity
Communication is the precise exchange of chunks of information (bits and bytes)	Communication is fluid, context-dependent, undetermined
Designers listen to the voice of customers	Designers develop an instinct for what customers want
Means and ends are clearly distinguished, and linked by a causal model	Means and ends cannot be clearly distinguished

These differences are so great that it seems impossible for someone to think interpretively and analytically at the same time. How can the two approaches be combined in practice?

A visit to Matsushita's product development laboratories outside Tokyo helped us to see, quite literally, how these two contradictory perspectives could be reconciled. At the entrance to the laboratories stands a display case containing all the cell phones that Matsushita's engineers have developed over the years. The display is arranged chronologically. At the left-hand end sits the first car phone—a massive, clunky device that looks hopelessly dated today. Stretching off to the right is a succession of progressively smaller instruments, ending with the tiniest phone that the company now has on the market. One way to look at this display is as a series of solutions to analytical problems. Each phone was the outcome of an engineering development project, with well-specified goals for size, weight, battery life, dialing functions, project lead-time, and so on. From this perspective we can see the progress of miniaturization and the trade-offs that were made between size and other engineering features at each stage. But looking at the display this way tells us almost nothing about how and why other aspects of the product evolved the way they did—why, for example, cell phone design evolved in the direction of fashion and style.

There is a different way to look at the display. From an interpretive viewpoint, each cell phone marks a stage in an ongoing, overlapping set of conversations between Matsushita and its customers and, internally, among the company's development engineers about the technical possibilities for cell phones and the ways in which they might be used. At each stage, the company makes a cell phone, passes it to the market, watches who buys it and how they use it, and then redesigns the phone so as to facilitate that use, drawing new consumers into the market in the process and encouraging existing customers to use the new phones in a slightly different way. These conversations at Matsushita are of course continuing, and the display case will acquire more new phones in the coming years, even though the broad direction of innovation is not clear today. The identity of the right-hand-most exhibit several years from now is anybody's guess.

Matsushita's display case is like a reel of celluloid film, in which the individual cell phones are frames. This metaphor helps us to see that product development is *both* analytical (the frames) and interpretive (the film). Like a motion picture and its still images, interpretation and analysis cannot be perceived simultaneously.

The idea that the same activity can be at once analytical and interpretive might seem illogical at first. But just as modern physics instructs us to think about light as both particles and waves, so too can a business organization be viewed from either the analytical or interpretive perspective.[1] As in the particle-wave duality, it is not accurate to say that the organization is either one thing or the other. Rather, it is both. One view may be more immediately useful in certain circumstances: as uncertainty increases, for example, the emphasis on interpretation should grow. But viewing the organization from both angles gives us deeper insight into what is going on, and this in turn opens up new possibilities for strategic behavior.

In our research, we observed many situations in which analytical and interpretive processes were taking place in the same firm, even though the practitioners themselves did not refer to them as such and often were not even aware of the distinction. Given the differences between the two processes, the difficulty of pursuing them simultaneously, and the challenge of sustaining them for the long term, how did these firms manage to pull it off?

Analysis, Interpretation, and the Product Lifecycle

Part of the answer is that at different times one approach becomes more important and receives more emphasis than the other. For example, while most product development organizations are engaged at any given moment in both analytical and interpretive activities, the balance shifts away from the interpretive as products mature. Most young product development groups evolve into more formal and structured organizations over time.

Early in the life of new products, firms find it possible—indeed preferable—to treat product development as an ad hoc collection of issues that can be dealt with in separate, loosely coordinated conversations with individual customers. It is during these conversations that developers come to understand more about the customer's environment and the product comes to be defined. But as the number of customers and the menu of technological options expands, the costs of this kind of customization—with its engineering overhead, long manufacturing cycle, and extra inventory—can quickly become unaffordable. So firms typically introduce a more systematic approach, with tighter control over schedules and the introduction of new features, as well as a more formal product planning process and organizational structure. Despite much contemporary managerial advice stressing the value of informality and porous organizational structures, most firms have no choice but to move in the opposite direction as they mature. The key question is not *whether* this should happen—it usually must—but *how*.

This evolution was clear in the cellular industry, and our research revealed that how it happened varied significantly among the leading firms. In the early stages of the industry, developers confronted a high degree of ambiguity and uncertainty about cellular systems and services. It was unclear initially whether the main market would be for car-mounted phones or handheld devices. It was also unclear how the various functions of the cellular system would be parceled out among the different system components (the central switch, the base station in each cell, and the phones themselves); whether cellular systems would use analog or digital technologies; if digital, which of several possible approaches; what alternative services could be delivered; who the potential customers were; what markets they would be found in; how much spectrum would be available; and which regulatory standards would prevail in each market.

Initially, each of the companies that have come to dominate the cellular industry managed this confusion of issues and ambiguities by using a highly interpretive approach—suspending formal decision-making procedures and encouraging open communication across organizational boundaries. Nokia's cellular business began as a highly entrepreneurial operation with informal design procedures. Sales-people communicated directly with the product development team, often making last-minute changes to product specifications in response to customers' requests. Motorola organized its initial efforts around a core of engineers who operated as a team, drawing in other members of the organization as required and conversing directly with customers about their needs and desired product features. Panasonic's (Matsushita's) cellular unit lacked clear functional boundaries, thus encouraging communication between its product-development and manufacturing units.

As we have already seen, AT&T housed its cellular operations in Bell Labs, a quasi-academic setting where radio and telephone engineers were insulated from the kind of market pressures that might have undermined early conversations. (It would later spin off these and other activities into Lucent Technologies.) Ericsson had neither a sheltered environment like Bell Labs nor an obvious organizational division in which to place early projects. Instead, it drew resources and personnel project-by-project from existing divisions and then tried to market its new products through those existing divisions. This approach created multiple conflicts and clashes.

As time went on, these open structures and interpretive processes proved to be increasingly costly to maintain. They led to a proliferation of special features and change orders that minimized the possibilities for reusing software code (the heart of cellular systems) and prolonged the time needed to bring a new product to market. Meanwhile, the main alternatives came into clearer focus, and the need to be engaged in many different open-ended discussions seemed to diminish. Europe's adoption of the digital GSM standard resolved a number of key system design issues, while the developing countries began to follow the regulatory standards of the major markets. A fairly well-defined set of alternative digital standards was gradually adopted around the world. Cost pressures led companies to question whether they could afford to be competing on all fronts simultaneously, and the sorting out of some of the technical ambiguities led them to wonder whether they really needed to. In effect, the companies chose to leave the cocktail-party phase of product development in order to make some hard-nosed business decisions about where to focus their efforts.

All of the companies followed this pattern, but the transition was most dramatic at AT&T. After it moved its cellular operations out of Bell Labs, the company established a stand-alone business unit, Network Wireless Systems (later spun off into Lucent), led by experienced managers drawn from other operating divisions and subject to the conventional AT&T bureaucratic practices and hierarchy.

Ericsson imposed a formal, bureaucratic structure as well. Although all of the cellular companies were conscious of the differences between the radio and telephone industries, Ericsson seemed obsessed with this cultural clash. It viewed the integration of radio and telephone engineering as the central management problem in bringing cell phones to market. The key to reform, in the company's eyes, was to impose the orderly and structured telephone culture upon the radio engineers and the cellular division as a whole. While Ericsson's new organizational structure was quite similar to AT&T's, it seemed to place much more emphasis on specialization. But then additional specialized units had to be created just to overcome the problems caused by the division of labor into specialized units. In other words, it created separate units whose specialty was integration—a process which seeks to overcome the drawbacks of specialization!

The company adopted a matrix management structure,

with projects as the profit centers. The projects in effect "hired" their personnel from the functional divisions. Projects were further divided into subprojects. The projects operated as groups, but the groups did not form into organic teams; each member of the group operated as much as possible in his or her own area of technical expertise. Integration was achieved by so-called systems people who specialized in the integration function and were chosen for their ability to "listen, learn, and talk" and to "persuade rather than direct." The project form of organization was supplemented by other specialized units with clear assignments: competency teams, which worked on specific problems spanning a number of different projects, and ad hoc experts, often PhD's, who were encouraged to roam the company looking for areas in which to apply their expertise. As at AT&T, communication in the cellular division, once it was restructured, consisted of the exchange of information rather than the cultivation of an interpretive community.

A similar though somewhat less drastic reorganization occurred at about the same time at Matsushita. The company made a decision to exit the infrastructure business altogether and to focus exclusively on the market for the telephone instrument. It reorganized its telephone business and brought in an experienced manager from its television division to oversee production. A clearly defined hand-off point between product development and manufacturing was instituted. The development engineers, who had previously themselves taken the new product into production, instead turned their designs over to production engineers, who subjected the designs to a series of tests of manufacturing feasibility before accepting them into mass production.

The chief difference between AT&T and Ericsson on the one hand and Matsushita on the other was an awareness at

Matsushita of the interpretive implications of its reorganization. The decision to exit the infrastructure business was in fact based partly on the company's inability to maintain the kind of conversational interactions it felt were necessary to remain competitive in that part of the business. Matsushita was particularly concerned that it did not manufacture its own switch. The cost of developing the capability to do so was judged to be prohibitive; and without some interaction between the switch designers and the engineers working on the rest of the infrastructure technology, the company could not acquire a good feel for that end of the business.

A second important consideration for Matsushita was the barriers to entry into the domestic infrastructure market in Japan. A third was the company's belief that it was being excluded from important conversations taking place in the regulatory domain in the American and European markets. Each of these factors figured in Matsushita's decision to drop its infrastructure business. But the executives we interviewed were extremely aware of critical interactions between infrastructure and the development of telephones. They worried that the decision to exit infrastructure had been a mistake, and they thought periodically of reentering that end of the business.

Motorola and Nokia also embraced a more analytical approach over time. But compared with the other three companies, both firms retained more of the original interpretive perspective after their reorganizations. At Motorola, the clash between the radio and telephone cultures was resolved by making a sharp distinction between hardware and software development and hiring an experienced manager from AT&T to direct the software division. This manager was also given responsibility for development as a whole—a move that effectively subordinated hardware (and radio) to the much more systematic processes associated with software and tele-phone. The newly hired executive restricted customers' access to the company's engineers and created the position of project manager to coordinate engineering efforts and to mediate relationships with the outside. The project manager became in effect a gatekeeper, controlling and limiting new commitments, and also a monitor, checking progress and ensuring that the company could meet its contractual timelines and budgets. This imported AT&T model met with resistance, however, and was eventually modified. In the model that emerged at Motorola, the project manager had much more limited decision-making authority; he became more of a consensus builder who initiated conversations among the various members of his team.

At Nokia, reorganization in the cell phone division began with the imposition of a gating process. Formal reviews were required in order for a design to pass through each gate. A clearly defined organizational chart designated responsibilities at each stage of the process. An overall project manager was installed, and individual project leaders were drawn from each major organizational area. Ideas about what new features a product should include were collected early on, but then the list was closed. After that point, if, for example, the marketing people rushed in to demand an additional feature that a competitor was about to introduce, it had to wait until the next product generation, or in the extreme case the existing development project would be killed and the process started *de novo*.

Despite this formality at Nokia—appearing at times to border on rigidity—our respondents placed considerable emphasis on the close integration of the company's product development teams. The project manager was described as operating like "the conductor of the orchestra, a guy who does not need special technical skills but needs a lot of common sense." The core design team of four people remained constant even as other specialists joined and left the project, and the company worked by consensus: "There is never a hand-off here. If everybody does not agree, the project does not go forward."

None of our respondents in the cellular industry were familiar with the analytical–interpretive distinction we make here, but the two firms (Motorola and Nokia) that retained more of the conversational, open-ended features of their early product development activities also seemed most aware of what was worth holding onto as they made the transition to a more formal structure.

Still, the instinct to adopt an analytical approach as a market matures was pervasive among cellular competitors. As a business grows larger and more complex, its efficiency depends on the establishment of well-defined operating processes and formal management structures. Strong problem-solving skills become more and more important to effective management. The value of having an interpretive–analytical framework in place during this transition is that it helps product development groups think more clearly about what they are giving up as they move toward a more formal organization. And it may also help them preserve within the maturing organization some of the virtues of the earlier, developmental phase of the business.

In the case of cellular, the advantage of preserving an interpretive perspective actually became clearer over time. When the companies began their shift from interpretive to analytical organizations, they shared a belief that the cellular business was stabilizing, with increasingly well-defined customer needs and product features. In hindsight, we can see that these expectations were inflated. The cellular business soon entered a new period of radical uncertainty. The introduction of personal communications service (PCS), the growing communications power of personal digital assistants and pagers, the expanding range of cordless phones, the increasing sophistication of satellite systems—all of these converged in a way that could not have been anticipated, again casting into doubt the role that traditional cellular service would ultimately play. Still more recently, the rapid emergence of wireless communications as a new channel to the Internet is creating a new wave of opportunities for the cellular industry, as well as a great deal of uncertainty about how consumers will actually use this capability. At present no one really knows how mobile Internet access will affect the range of wireless services and the kinds of wireless devices that consumers will want.

Analysis, Interpretation, and the Corporate Lifecycle

As the cellular industry demonstrates, a lot can be learned about the informal-to-formal transition in product development organizations if we look at it through the two lenses of interpretation and analysis. But on a larger scale, what can this approach teach us about the periodic company-wide restructurings that growing firms undergo in an attempt to manage the problems of increasing size? Consider the case of Lutron, which in its early years was a single highly integrated organization. But as its product lines crystallized and matured, and with sales doubling every three or four years, the company eventually felt compelled to divide itself into a set of business units dedicated to particular product lines. This led to a problem that many other companies also experience: *silos* within the organization, in which people are increasingly thinking about their product lines in isolation from the rest of the business. The problem appeared to be structural, caused by the formation of business units based on specific products, and thus seemed to require a structural solution. Either the business units would have to be abandoned in favor of a different organizational architecture, or they would have to be supplemented with cross-cutting units charged with sales, research and development, customer service, and so on.

Another way to look at the problem, however, is that the reorganization divided the company into conversational groups, just as a cocktail party breaks up into many smaller groupings as more and more guests arrive. Over time, as people become preoccupied with the conversation in their own group, it becomes more and more difficult for people in different groups to talk with one another. From this perspective, it is not clear that an alternative organizational form will solve the underlying problem—that the company is now just too large to sustain a single conversation. A reorganization would simply split it into a different set of groups that would also be at risk of turning inward on themselves.

When the problem is viewed in this way, as an interpretive problem, what is required is to enlarge the conversation within the groups and to stimulate conversation among them. This is difficult to do because people from the different groups tend to meet most often in adversarial situations when they are competing for budgetary resources or the attention of the sales organization they share. Even so, specific measures can be taken to guide the conversations—for example, by rotating personnel among the groups, by sponsoring intracompany forums and events, and so on. Oticon, the Danish hearing aid company, actually redesigned the physical layout of its offices, removing walls and reconfiguring corridors and work spaces, to ensure physical interaction among people in the course of the day who might otherwise be confined to their separate silos.

It is important to recognize that the problem of silos cannot be made to go away. The problem *is* structural. And as long as the structure that the company has chosen exists, it will require a managerial approach that is analytical—a manager who can mediate the conflicts among the organizational units and, if necessary, make the choices among their competing claims in light of the best interest of the organization as a whole.

If, however, the manager views the company *only* through an analytical lens, he is likely to just keep looking for different ways to divide up the organization. At Lutron, for example, in addition to the product-based structure that was eventually adopted, managers actively considered both a technology-based and a market-based architecture. But while certain structures may have inherent advantages, none will ever be quite right. On the other hand, if managers adopt an interpretive perspective on the problem of silos, a broad range of organizational structures can be made to work.

Simultaneous Analytical and Interpretive Processes

Most firms face the challenge of moving through the product lifecycle, and on a longer time-scale the corporate lifecycle, without completely abandoning the open, informal, conversational character of their early product development activities. And as we have seen, the interpretive–analytical framework provides a valuable perspective on how to achieve these transitions. But many firms also seek to field a portfolio of products in the marketplace, some of them mature and others less so, and they must contend with what in many ways is an even greater challenge: to pursue the interpretive and analytical approaches to product development *simultaneously.*

Levi's prepares "collections" for its major product lines several times a year. The company thinks of these in terms of a V-shaped merchandising model. Merchandising in the garment industry is distinguished from marketing; it concerns the way in which store space is utilized and the product is presented to the consumer at the point of sale. At the back of the store are the standard items, the backbone of the collection which generates the bulk of the company's revenues. These items change little from year to year. At the very front of the store are new items aimed at the fashion-conscious consumer and often geared to a particular season. In the middle are a set of items introduced in earlier collections that have sold well but have not yet earned a place in the company's permanent collection. Products move from the front of the store to the back over their lifecycle, and they may be dropped from the collection at any time.

In many ways Levi's method of preparing its collections is consistent with the analytical mode of product development. The effort is organized in a series of distinct phases. There are definite start and end dates, and there are "gates" through which the collection has to pass as it moves toward the market. Fashion apparel tends to follow a standard S-shaped epidemic (or contagion) model. Aggressive marketing and merchandising can sometimes alter a trajectory, but once a design has been introduced and has spent some time on store shelves, its fate can be predicted fairly accurately, and decisions about it can be structured analytically based on hard data.

For the newest fashion items at the front of the store, however, the analytical approach will not work. There is simply too much uncertainty about fashion trends, customer reactions, and even manufacturing capabilities. At the time of our interviews, Levi's managed the design and development of these items very differently from the way it managed the collection as a whole, and the approach had an important interpretive dimension. While Levi's did not assign product development for the latest fashions to a separate organization, several respondents in our interviews drew a distinction between the designers who generated fashion innovations and those whose strength was in the execution of ideas generated by others.

Other firms, facing a similar challenge, try to create a separate space within the company where interpretive activities can occur. In our research we saw two broad solutions to this problem. One was to carve out such a space within the company itself. The crudest and most straightforward way is to permanently insulate an enclave from the economic pressures that govern behavior in the rest of the company. Bell Labs and the Cardinal unit at Lutron are prototypes for this solution. The second approach is to modify organizational structures more generally, so as to soften their analytical edge and encourage the open-ended conversations that are critical to interpretation. Nokia did this by requiring that a decision to proceed at each stage of a product's development had to be unanimous; if someone did not agree with the rest of the group, then everyone continued to talk through the group's differences of opinion.

An alternative to these internally focused strategies is to place the company at the intersection of a conversational community that spans a number of different enterprises. One example from our case studies is the strategy pursued by Intel (discussed briefly in Chapter 3).[2] Intel's primary product was (and still is) the microprocessor for personal computers. Technological development in the industry—which Intel leads—is such that the microprocessor has doubled in processing power roughly every year and a half. (This phenomenon is known as Moore's Law, after an observation made by Gordon Moore, one of Intel's founders, in 1965.) That progression has required the resolution of a series of technological problems which for the most part have been addressed analytically. But technological advance is only viable economically if the new generation of chips is incorporated into computer-based products that the consumer is interested in buying. And the consumer is only interested in trading up if there are attractive software and peripheral hardware products that cannot run on older computers.

The number and variety of such products, and the uncertainty about the market for any one of them, are too great for Intel itself to develop and produce them. Instead, it encourages a population of often much smaller firms working around it to engage in this development. But in the early stages there are so many unknowns that the interfaces between the various components cannot be codified. So in order to ensure that Intel's new chip and the peripheral products are compatible, Intel and at least some of the outsider firms must have a way to engage in constant interaction. That interaction, we suggested earlier, is an example of a conversation that Intel has to organize.

The organizational problem Intel faces is created by the temptation of competition. Through its interactions with smaller firms, Intel acquires enough technical knowledge of the peripherals to produce any one of them itself and hence compete directly with the very firms it needs as collaborators. Were Intel to succumb to this temptation, those firms would no longer have an interest in developing products to support the market for Intel's chip. Intel's organizational solution is to decree that decisions about peripheral product development can be made only at the highest management level, by the company president, who is presumably in a position to weigh the less tangible but very real benefits of ongoing conversations with collaborators against the immediate profits that might accrue from producing a peripheral product in-house.

The jeans industry provides another example where firms have created or exploited multifirm conversational spaces. Martelli, the laundry located in the Veneto region of Italy, sees its clients, its competitors, and its suppliers all as critical parts of its network. Its relationship with Tornello, a maker of washing machines and other finishing equipment located in the same region, is particularly close. Martelli advises Tornello about what effects it is trying to achieve, Tornello tests its new equipment in Martelli's facilities, and Martelli evaluates the results for Tornello in terms of their likely impact upon the marketability of different fabrics. Martelli in turn lets Tornello bring potential clients to see the company's equipment in operation in Martelli's facilities; because of Martelli's worldwide reputation, this is an important sales tool for Tornello. But because Tornello's people sell equipment throughout the world and travel widely to install and service it, the company is also a source of far-flung market intelligence.

Martelli also seeks to work for a number of competing jeans manufacturers in order to stretch its creative imagination about what is possible technologically and at the cutting edge stylistically. At the time of our interviews, the firm was finishing jeans for the two leading Italian jeans companies, Diesel and Replay, as well as several major American brands. But at least some of these customers were fearful that their new styles would leak, through Martelli, to their competitors. Martelli handled the problem by dedicating physically separate facilities, each with its own managerial structure, to each of its major clients. Only a small group of top managers, engineers, and designers at Martelli dealt with all of its customers at the same time and were thus exposed to the full range of developments in the industry. The top management group was small enough to preserve confidentiality (and, more to the point, make it credible to the client) but large enough to permit a creative conversation within Martelli itself. New finishing ideas that emerged from this internal conversation were shared with customers on a very selective basis, in a strategy designed to maintain the client's interest and incentive to work with Martelli despite the risks.

The same fear of information leakage that led Martelli to separate the management of its relationships with the different jeans brands and to handle them in separate facilities led Levi's to insist that all its laundries work for it exclusively. Levi's supplier network was quite extensive. The company operated its own laundries and laboratories but also used a number of outside contractors for finishing, including American Garment Finishers of El Paso. Levi's managers believed that the contract laundries, because of their wider networks, were better placed to bring new ideas for finishing to the table and were often the first to try out new finishing equipment. But because of concerns about the leakage of information to its competitors, Levi's also had a policy of developing exclusive relationships with its contractors.

At the time of our initial interviews, American Garment Finishers had just entered into an exclusive relationship with Levi's. Its president, Claude Blankiet, was in the process of winding down his firm's contracts with other jeans manufacturers. Over the years, Blankiet had developed an extensive network of contacts in the industry across Asia, Europe, and the United States that helped him stay on top of technical developments. He combined formal training as a chemical engineer with a strong intuitive sense for fashion and design honed through years of experience in the industry. He moved easily between the highly technical world of the laundries and the commercial and fashion-oriented world of the designers. His clients at Levi's as well as other interviewees around the industry credited him with exceptional judgment about the marketability of new effects achieved in the finishing process.

Both Martelli and Tornello were close collaborators of Blankiet, and in interviews with us they expressed great skepticism about Blankiet's new exclusive relationship with Levi's. They were obviously concerned, both for him and for themselves, that in taking this step Blankiet's range of contacts was becoming too thin. But Blankiet's view was that product development at Levi's had suffered from the insularity and isolation of the different laundry facilities, and he saw his role as strengthening communication among the laundry facilities within the company and at other contractors. Although these facilities regularly encountered similar technical problems in achieving each desired new finish, they shared little information about how to resolve them, partly because Levi's had tended to treat its own laundries as competitors. This was also acknowledged by the Levi's product development managers, but they wanted Blankiet to work out a technical solution and then standardize the knowledge and procedures across Levi's network of laundries—in essence, they viewed this as an analytical problem.

Blankiet's understanding of his new role was different. He saw himself as continuing to do inside the company what he had previously done across the industry: instigate conversations among laundries and interpret for people who initially are not speaking the same language. He sought not so much to eliminate variations in finishing but rather to exploit those variations as a continuing source of new fashion ideas and insights. His efforts to do this were resisted, at least initially, by other managers in the Levi's network, who valued the exchange of information but did not appreciate the interpretive dimension of the process.

Shortly after we completed our interviews, Levi's jeans began to lose their cachet on the street fashion scene. It is difficult to say whether the company's decisions regarding the organization of its supply network were a contributing factor. What is clear, though, is that Levi's managers saw the networking issue almost entirely in analytical terms, and they lacked the interpretive vocabulary that might have led them to adopt a more open networking strategy. Indeed, not only did they see Blankiet's role within the Levi's network primarily as one of problem solving and standardization, but they also expected it to be short-term. Despite having the highest regard for Blankiet's skills, they saw his internal networking activities as a temporary expedient that would be needed only as long as the technology of finishing retained its ad hoc, empirical character.

At some point, they believed, finishing technology, then still an inexact science, would acquire a firmer theoretical foundation. The long-run solution would be to hire, or grow, designers cross-trained in chemistry or chemical engineering, who would be able to analyze the feasibility of the designs they were recommending and express their technical solutions as written formulas that could be passed from one laundry to another electronically. This would obviate the need for the kinds of face-to-face communication networks Blankiet had spent his career cultivating and which he was planning to build across Levi's internal laundry complex. In this conception of the supply network, little value was attached to the ongoing conversations and debates among laundries, machine manufacturers, and others that Blankiet and his Italian colleagues believed was an important source of new ideas.

The continuing hold of the analytical model on thinking about product development in the denim jeans sector is particularly striking because the relevance of interpretive approaches to fashion has been extensively discussed in the literature on the fashion industry. Indeed, at Levi's itself we found other aspects of product development that quite clearly were interpretive in character, even if the practitioners themselves did not use that term to describe them. But in the case of the laundry network, the lack of an interpretive vocabulary did seem to limit the ways that managers thought about their organizational options. From a purely analytical perspective, the benefits of having more ideas flowing in from the outside must be weighed against the risks of proprietary information leaking out to competitors. But this calculation leaves no room for the intersecting conversations within and among communities from which new ideas emerge. For the managers at Levi's, the default to analytical thinking was locking the company into a zero-sum game.

The Need for Public Space

Our research revealed a variety of strategies for creating spaces for interpretive activity. It is hard to escape the conclusion, however, that these interpretive spaces are fragile, even those that are created within a firm. The Cardinal unit at Lutron was eventually dismantled after it corrupted its interpretive mission by attempting to become an independent profit center.[3] When AT&T's cell phone business was moved out of the sheltered environment of Bell Labs, critical interpretive dimensions of the managerial structure were irretrievably lost.[4] The conversational space that Intel created with the producers of peripheral products was under such pressure from within the company to produce the most profitable items internally that these decisions had to be preserved for the very highest levels of management. Martelli's customers were so fearful of losing trade secrets to competitors that the company had to restrict its interpretive conversation, which drew on experience from a cross-section of clients, to a handful of top managers. The same fears caused Levi's to try to cut off such conversations completely.

The fragility of these interpretive spaces is not solely attributable to the cognitive difficulty of pursuing two contradictory management styles at the same time, although that is surely a factor. The interpretive process is also inherently in conflict with the economic environment in which business operates. Interpretation involves cooperation, transparency, and disclosure. It also demands a degree of trust that your interlocutor is not deliberately trying to deceive you. Economic competition, on the other hand, fosters opportunism, secrecy, and confidentiality. It creates an environment of suspicion and *dis*trust. In an economic organization, interpretation is understandably pushed to the margin. Many of the management styles and business structures that we have discussed are therefore less about how to create the interactions around which interpretation takes place than they are about staving off the economic pressures that inhibit its growth.

These competitive obstacles both within and among firms suggest the need for public spaces within which free-flowing conversations can occur. But such spaces are not easily created or maintained. They pose the classic free-rider problem. The dilemma is best illustrated by the one company in our study that seemed most dependent on public space, the French women's clothing chain Camaïeu. Camaïeu had no internal design capacity. Instead, its buyers collected a series of designs from small firms in Sentier, the garment district of

Paris. It displayed these in a group of its own test stores and then analyzed sales. The strongest-selling items were mass-produced for the rest of Camaïeu's sales outlets. The small firms responsible for the original design usually did not have the capacity to produce the requisite quantities, so the bulk of production was subcontracted to manufacturers outside of Sentier, often abroad.

Camaïeu had in effect cut off or externalized the interpretive part of the product development process. The company was a passive intermediary—a good listener, perhaps, but certainly not the active conversationalist that Levi's sought to be in the case of, for example, baggy jeans. Camaïeu was completely dependent upon the small community of producers in Sentier to generate the styles that it tested in its stores. Its relationship to Sentier was parasitic. It did nothing to support the interpretive processes there that generated the designs which it sold, and in fact it had no economic incentive to do so.

How then do public spaces arise? How should we think about their contribution to the interpretive process? We turn to these questions in the next chapter.

PUBLIC SPACE

6

In new product development, interpretation and analysis exist in perpetual tension. This tension is inevitable and unavoidable, and we believe it is the central management problem that innovative businesses must confront. The tension, as we have seen, springs from many sources. Interpretation proceeds through conversations over time—within and among the various communities that contribute to new product development and between the designers and the customers who use those new products and incorporate them into their lives. Analysis, on the other hand, takes place "outside of time"—at the point when a product must be optimized according to well-defined and articulated objectives. Financial gains are easily jeopardized by premature disclosure of innovations to competitors, and the fear of such disclosures can lead to secrecy and withdrawal from ongoing conversations. A breakdown in communication is particularly likely in the early stages of innovation, when the participants in the process do not share a language that would allow them to isolate ambiguity and to distinguish between genuine misunderstanding and opportunism.

Public spaces can help businesses manage the tension between analysis and interpretation. They provide a venue in which new ideas and insights can emerge, without the risk that private appropriation of information will undermine or truncate the discussion. In our case studies, we encountered four critical types of public space:

- The interior of the firm itself
- Industrial districts
- The regulatory process
- The university

Of these, the university is the institution with which we are directly concerned and most familiar, and we devote Chapter 7 to an examination of the threats now facing universities as public spaces. In this chapter, we recapitulate some of the incentives and disincentives that arise when managers attempt to set up public spaces within the private sector—whether within individual firms or industrial districts. This section is followed by a lengthier discussion of regulation—a kind of public forum that has become the focus of active policy debate.

The media and the arts comprise a fifth public space that we have touched on in other chapters but will not discuss at length. The fashion industry is particularly dependent on larger cultural trends, exchanges, and outlets for expression. But other products we studied cannot be completely understood without reference to the role of the media and the arts. Cell phones, for example, have become a fashion item in some important respects. In promoting its anesthesia-monitoring device, Aspect (following a common strategy in the drug industry) produced an extensive public relations campaign to educate the public about the after-effects of anesthesia. And Chiron's viral load measuring devices could not have been marketed as effectively had the broad-based public discussion of AIDS never taken place.

The Firm as a Public Space

In a sense, Chapters 4 and 5, which focus on ways that businesses can better manage the inherent tensions of the analytical–interpretive dichotomy, can also be read as a commentary on the difficulty of maintaining public space within a private enterprise. From a broad socioeconomic perspective, we can see that this tension has increased in recent decades as competitive pressures have been applied in every part of the economy.

For much of the twentieth century, the economy was populated by large, oligopolistic companies that were sheltered in one way or another from competition. The origins of those companies is a matter of some debate; but they do not seem to have been created as a response to a need for interpretive space.[1] Nevertheless, whether by accident or design, a major consequence was the emergence of spaces within these firms where interpretation could flourish. The great industrial R&D labs at IBM, DuPont, and General Electric are leading examples.

Over the last twenty years, two developments have changed the character of these public spaces within private enterprise. One is the movement to break down organizational barriers within large firms. The second is the increasing competitive pressures acting on them. The major result of the first has been to improve communication between the sheltered spaces and the rest of the company—an enduring problem under the older structure. An extreme example was the relationship of Xerox to its Palo Alto Research Center (PARC). In its most profitable years, Xerox taxed itself heavily to create a research laboratory. The lab was located in Palo Alto, close to the high-technology community there, whose unfettered ideas and dynamic culture the company hoped to absorb. PARC was a prolific source of new computing and communications products, including the personal computer, local area networks, the graphical user interface, laser printers, and the mouse. But its location was so distant physically and socially from Xerox's commercial operations and headquarters on the East Coast that ideas circulating at PARC never seemed to reach the rest of the company, and the products that PARC developed were ultimately commercialized not by Xerox but by other Silicon Valley start-ups.[2]

Most large American companies have been shrinking or dismantling their central research labs over the past decade and redirecting their remaining R&D activity toward the shorter-term product development needs of their business units. Insofar as this lowers the boundaries between the conversational spaces for R&D and the company's operating divisions, these reforms have a salutary effect on the interpretive process. But the principal consequence of breaking down these barriers has been to expose previously sheltered enclaves to greater competitive pressure.

Globalization, technological change, and the deregulation of many industries account for much of this revved-up competition, but these external factors have been amplified by internal compensation and promotion incentives. Underlying both internal reforms and external pressures, especially from deregulation, is the highly articulated ideology of market competition. Under its influence, even reforms that were initially intended to reduce internal barriers to communication and the flow of ideas have come to be understood as responses to competitive pressure. As a result, they have been implemented in a way that reduces the extent of previously sheltered conversational spaces and requires these conversations to be evaluated in analytical terms. The spin-off and commercialization of Bell Labs is a prominent example, but similar reforms have occurred in other commercial laboratories like those of DuPont and IBM.

Industrial Districts as Public Spaces

This term originated with Alfred Marshall in the early twentieth century.[3] It described groupings of small firms that together form an industrial community whose technical and commercial foundations are, as Marshall put it, in the very air that is breathed. In recent literature, the term has been extended to cover Silicon Valley, high-fashion garment districts in New York and Paris, and towns in central Italy specializing in products ranging from fashion shoes and textiles to motorbikes and customized packaging equipment.[4] Whether their products are waistcoats or widgets, such districts are basically interpretive communities. The knowledge and understanding circulating from firm to firm have the properties of a language and evolve through conversation.

Most of the industrial districts that have been well studied seem to have emerged naturally, and they have proved to be very difficult to replicate through deliberate public policy. They are also difficult to sustain. Like interpretive spaces within a firm, industrial districts have been subject to enormous pressures in recent decades.[5] One disruptive pressure comes from large firms that draw on the knowledge base of these communities while contributing little to support them. The relationship between Camaïeu and Sentier in Paris is typical of the kind of exploitation one sees in the Italian high fashion industry and among Brazilian shoe manufacturers.[6] Other responses to these pressures—also notable in central Italy—have been constructed. In response to the threat of external competition and sometimes the defection of larger companies, the districts have become increasingly self-conscious. They have created internal governance structures that try to conserve and enrich the conversational process and orient it strategically.[7]

Large firms sometimes emerge as the leaders of industrial districts. Among clothing manufacturers, Benetton—in the Veneto region of Italy—has played this role. But as Intel's relationship with small peripherals firms illustrates, competitive pressures constrain this leadership role and threaten it, just as they do the sheltered conversational spaces within large companies.

The rapid development of the Internet over the past decade is giving the term *industrial districts* a very contemporary cast. New kinds of public spaces are emerging within whose virtual boundaries multitudes of economic actors engage with one another, unconstrained by geography. Among the most notable are the open source software communities that have grown up online and are now mounting a serious challenge to proprietary software developers in some important markets. The well-known Linux operating system and the Apache web server software are just the tip of the iceberg for open source projects.

The essential feature of open source software is that it is not owned in the conventional sense. It is freely available, not just to the members of the online communities but to anyone at all. The code is not actually given away, and a system of well-defined rights and obligations surrounding its use prevents it from entering the public domain. But this system of sharing is radically different from the intellectual property regime governing conventional proprietary software.

Software may be very expensive to develop initially, but it costs almost nothing to reproduce. The problem for commercial software developers, therefore, is how to keep control of their product and therefore the revenue stream it produces. They achieve this by preventing their customers from reproducing, modifying, and redistributing the software, partly through copyright, patent, and license restrictions and partly through trade secrets—concealing the underlying source code, without which modifications are typically extremely difficult to make.

In the case of open source, all this is turned on its head. Members of open software communities must distribute the source code along with any code they have developed. Anyone is permitted to redistribute the software at no charge, without paying royalties to the original author. Any user may also modify the software, but he is obligated to make the modifications generally available along with their source code, and access cannot be denied to any subsequent users (although developers can charge fees for use, or for ancillary services that they package along with the code). The system is thus designed to ensure that the fundamental rights to use, modify, and redistribute software propagate indefinitely, throughout all subsequent generations of code and users. Whereas conventional intellectual property restricts the commons, the aim of open source is to expand it.[8]

In the terms of our interpretive-analytical framework, open source communities obviously have a strong analytical dimension. Open software, like any computer code, is essentially made up of solutions to well-defined analytical problems. But the members of these communities are also continuously involved in intense interpretive discussions concerning, for example, what is wrong with existing software and how it might be improved, why a particular piece of code works well, what constitutes an elegant solution, what would be a good new feature, and so on. (The members almost never meet face-to-face, and these conversations mostly take place online.)

A typical open source project spans many kinds of organizational boundaries. Informal surveys indicate that the majority of members work for business firms. But the key point is that the communities are open and membership is voluntary; people can and do enter and leave at any time, and they are free to choose what problem or code feature to work on. It is typical for multiple approaches to the same issue to be pursued in parallel in a given project. There is no central coordination of tasks in the conventional sense, although pieces of code that are incorporated into the core of the software must pass through a formal approval mechanism. (In the case of Linux, that mechanism until fairly recently was the approval of the original author, the Finnish software engineer Linus Torvalds.)

Many observers have been surprised by the durability of open software communities, especially given that most developers are not compensated for their work and given also the ever-present threat of code "forks," which arise when developers split off from a project and begin developing a portion of the code independently—a problem that beset the earlier generation of UNIX operating systems. But the open source movement has been gaining strength; tens of thousands of developers and users now participate, and a growing number of large companies, including IBM, Hewlett-Packard, and Oracle, have embraced the approach for some of the software they produce. One of the benefits perceived by these companies is the opportunity to tap into the creative and problem-solving abilities of the user base—a resource that is mostly inaccessible to the developers of proprietary software.

The development of open software has until now been a grassroots phenomenon, with little or no encouragement at the policy level. But as open source code becomes more widespread and increasingly intermingled with proprietary code, a collision between these two radically different ways of organizing software production seems almost inevitable, with the users' rights asserted under the open source system pitted against the rights of developers that are protected by conventional proprietary licenses. How such a clash would be resolved is far from clear.

The very existence of open software suggests a set of unexpected and unexplored forces generating public space within the private sector. Given the way in which that space is otherwise narrowing, it is a model which we clearly need to understand and if necessary encourage through public policy. There is no indication, however, that that model could provide a general solution to the difficulties of preserving public space within the private sector of a competitive economy. This, then, points to the importance of spaces that are explicitly public.

Regulation at the FCC

In our case studies, the regulatory arena emerged clearly as a public space in American society where interpretive conversation takes place. This finding implies an economic role for the regulatory process quite different from that which has dominated the debate about regulation and deregulation over the last quarter century.

The role of regulation as public space was initially highlighted in our interviews with Matsushita. One of the key moments in the evolution of Matsushita's strategy, as we have seen, was the decision to withdraw from the cellular infrastructure business and concentrate solely on the production and distribution of telephone instruments. In taking this path, the company departed from the other major cellular producers that we interviewed. The decision haunted the executives who made it, and they returned to it periodically in the course of our interviews, occasionally even suggesting that they were considering reversing direction and reentering the infrastructure business.

Their regrets centered on the fact that the telephone instrument and the infrastructure form an integrated system whose components are intricately interconnected. It is difficult to understand and anticipate the technological developments that are driving the evolution of the instrument itself if one is not actually involved in the development of the larger system into which it must fit. But the company felt that it could not compete effectively in the infrastructure business outside of Japan. And here its major competitive handicap was the fact that it had been excluded from the advisory committees of the Federal Communications Commission (FCC) in the United States.

At first we found this very hard to understand because the parameters of the FCC regulations are not set by the advisory committees. Indeed, since the United States—in contrast with the European Union—had decided not to establish a single cellular standard, the role of the FCC was largely confined to reserving a certain part of the radio spectrum for cellular and administering the auctions through which that spectrum was allocated to particular carriers. The regulations, moreover, were a matter of public record once they had been promulgated; in fact, proposals became public long before they went into effect.

In light of Matsushita's angst, we initially assumed that the companies participating in the advisory committees were able to use the regulatory process to gain some advantage for their own proprietary technologies. But ultimately it became clear that what concerned the Matsushita executives was the difficulty of *interpreting* the regulations without participating in the advisory discussions. They believed that U.S. producers developed an understanding of how the technology would evolve under a given regulatory regime that those on the outside could not develop on their own; and without this understanding, Matsushita could not hope to penetrate the U.S. market. They viewed Matsushita's exclusion from the conversations surrounding the U.S. regulatory process as a major nontariff barrier to trade.

For us, the story underscored the fact that the regulatory process had become a public, conversational space, one that is perhaps especially important in a competitive economy like that of the United States, where direct conversations among producers are limited by antitrust regulation and by competitive pressures. But what exactly was the advantage of being part of the regulatory conversation? What precisely did Matsushita lose by being excluding from direct participation in the regulatory process? Here we were not very successful in eliciting specific examples from our respondents at the company. Additional insights into the role of interpretation in the regulatory process did emerge, however, from two other sources. One was the relationship between chip development at Intel and the community of peripheral developers on the outside. The other was the effect of the standards adopted by the European Union on the cellular industry itself.

The problem at Intel, it will be recalled, is that the company has been introducing a new (and more powerful) microprocessor for personal computers roughly every 18 months, along the trajectory predicted by Moore's Law. In order to create a market for the computers that embody this increased capacity (and hence for "Intel inside"), new peripherals must be developed which depend upon this new capacity and which the consumers want to use. Because the peripherals must be compatible with the microprocessor, the designs are interdependent, and it would be natural to design them in sequence. If this was actually the way the design process occurred, the Intel design would be viewed by the peripheral developers as a constraint upon their own work, and one might think of Intel as "regulating" the peripheral industry, imposing its rules on their behavior.

But a sequential design process of this kind would take too long. By the time the peripherals arrived on the market the microprocessor would already be obsolete, replaced by a design with twice as much capacity. The chip and the peripheral designs must co-evolve so that a compatible set of products arrives at the market at the same time. To make this happen, Intel, as we have seen, orchestrates a conversation between its own developers and those on the outside.

So, returning to Matsushita, one way of understanding that company's exclusion from U.S. regulatory discussions is that it deprived top managers of participation in this co-evolution phase. Because it was barred from the conversation, the company could not anticipate the rules that would constrain its future behavior. It could have conformed to those rules after the fact, once they had been established, but it would have been in a position comparable to that of a peripheral developer that starts work after it actually sees what Intel's final chip design looks like. That company's products would always enter the market one step too late. To draw an analogy with the fashion industry, Matsushita was forced by its outsider status to always produce last year's styles. In cellular, as in fashion, there is a place for such producers, but the companies occupying that position are more like commodity producers. They do not lead the industry in the way that Matsushita sought to lead its industry, and they do not reap the supranormal profits.

Yet another way to think about the benefits of participating directly in the conversations surrounding the regulatory process is suggested by the experience in Europe with standardization of the cellular industry. In direct contrast to the United States, European regulators sought to develop a series of standard interfaces among the various components of the cellular infrastructure.[9] In principle, this meant that customers could build their own systems, combining, for example, a Nokia base station with an Ericsson switch and a Motorola base station controller.

Despite this modular approach, however, the standards fell short of producing interchangeability. It was possible to get a system up and running in this way, but such hybrids proved very difficult to maintain. When problems emerged, it was extremely expensive (or impossible) to troubleshoot them. Evidently, within the framework of standards prescribed by the regulatory authority, each company developed its own approach. The standards themselves left a range of ambiguity, and each of the producers had resolved that ambiguity in its own particular way. Each company had, in a sense, developed its own *interpretation;* and to understand it, you needed to be an insider, participating directly in the development. If this was true of companies that had actually participated in making the rules and hence had begun from a common starting point, imagine how much more difficult it would be for a company that started at one remove and had only the formal rules themselves to work with, as was the case of Matsushita in the U.S. market.

Regulations, this suggests, are like a language—a set of rules and perhaps a vocabulary as well which create an ambiguous space for interpretation. The companies that are absent from the process in which regulations are developed and evolve over time are like foreigners trying to understand a native speaker. Can they understand? Yes, of course. But perhaps never as fast or with the facility of a native.

Regulation at the FDA

Medical devices present a sharp contrast with the cellular case. The medical devices industry in the United States is regulated by the Food and Drug Administration (FDA), and FDA approval is required before a new device can be marketed. The FDA also limits the claims that may be made for the device in all advertising and sales campaigns. Approval is typically based on a series of blind, randomized trials which test both the safety and the efficacy of the product. The whole design and development process is oriented toward obtaining this approval, and as a result the regulatory process permeates the industry.

But the regulatory agency and the private firms seeking its approval operate at arms length. The approval process is informed by scientific advisory committees whose members are drawn primarily from the academic community. Interactions between the advisory committees and the applicants are indirect. The applicant provides the experimental evidence upon which approval is supposed to be based and responds to queries about the evidence that the agency staff or the advisory committee submits. The outcome is not necessarily determined by the evidence alone, however. Approval is often dependent upon the judgment of the committees (and ultimately the FDA and its staff) about how to weigh the benefits of the new device against the risks of adverse effects. More recently, the effects of devices on the cost of medical care—the length of hospital stay, for example, or the comparative cost of alternative treatments—have also been a factor in these decisions.

In the particular case of Aspect's BIS index, one of the claimed advantages was that with more precise estimates of the amount of anesthesia required, the recovery period and hence the time in intensive care would be reduced. The discussion of the alternative costs and benefits of a product and how they should be weighed, however, takes place entirely within the advisory committees and/or among the FDA staff. It does not involve a broader interaction (and certainly not an ongoing conversation) with the private developers, whose motives the regulators view with deep suspicion. Our interviews suggested that that suspicion was not unwarranted. The companies (or at least those with whom we talked) were focused almost exclusively upon gaining FDA approval and virtually never mentioned the underlying values (or goals) which the approval process was designed to serve.

The discussion of these goals and how they should be balanced against one another does take place in the broader political (or at least the congressional) arena, where the costs of regulatory delays and the risks of premature approval have been the subject of active debate in recent years. In the case of AIDS drugs, there is also an organized, militant, and knowledgeable constituency of consumers who have interacted with the regulatory agency and the pharmaceutical companies.[10] And that interaction has had the kind of continuity and intensity that might be termed a conversation. But this is extremely rare—in fact, it is probably unique.

For the most part, the actors in the regulatory process are limited to the agency and the companies developing the drugs and devices. They communicate with each other, to the extent they communicate at all, through a layer of private consultants. The consultants are typically lawyers and ex-FDA officials who act primarily as translators or interpreters of FDA regulations. They sometimes meet with FDA officials in special seminars or at professional congresses, but they do not interact with either their clients or the agency in anything approaching the give-and-take of an open-ended conversation. Moreover, the FDA-imposed rules which limit the claims that the company can make in sales and advertising actually structure (and limit) the kinds of conversations that developers can have with the medical community and with the consumers (or patients) who are ultimately treated with their products.

The development strategy in medical devices is to put a new product into the hands of clinicians and to get them to "play" with it, experimenting with ways it can be calibrated by their clinical experience and integrated into clinical practice. Thus, as we have seen, Aspect wanted anesthesiologists to use its monitoring device in the operating room as they administered anesthesia, and gradually to come to rely on the readings of the BIS index instead of their own observation of the patient. Chiron wanted doctors to use its viral load measure in combination with experimental AIDS drugs as they tried to adapt complex therapies to the needs of individual patients, in the hope that the viral load measures would come to substitute for clinical observations of the patient's condition. But in both cases, the claims that the companies were allowed to make in their published material—and actually in their verbal sales pitches as well—and the suggestions they could make to their clients about how to use the equipment even after it was in their hands were monitored and controlled closely by the FDA.

Explaining the Contrast

What explains the contrast between the FCC in cellular and the FDA in medical devices? When does regulation operate to facilitate the interpretive process and when does it act to inhibit it? How might the interpretive role of the regulatory process be fostered?

One way to think about the regulatory process is that, like product development itself, it encompasses two moments. One moment is essentially interpretive in character, the other analytical. The interpretive phase comes in the formulation of the regulations; the analytical phase comes when they are applied. These moments naturally follow sequentially in time. Because we observed the cellular industry early in its evolution, when the product was new and its nature unclear, the regulatory process was in its interpretive phase. In medical devices, the particular products upon which our case study focused were new, but the industry itself was long established and the regulatory procedures were well developed.

Of course in practice, regulations continue to be formulated even when the industry is mature, and hence one can discern two processes at each point in time. This suggests that in regulation, as in product development itself, the critical problem is how to maintain the interpretive process and manage it in the later states of the lifecycle, when regulations are also being applied and administered.

The distinction between the formulation of the regulations and their administration is clearest when the regulations consist of a bureaucratic set of rules and procedures that leave little room for discretion in their administration. Here, the analogy to the product development process as we have characterized it is actually quite strong. The promulgation of a set of regulations is generally preceded by a process in which the need for regulation is discussed and various interested parties try to understand what exactly is at stake in the regulatory arena, what the society is trying to achieve, what technical and social forces are impinging on that achievement, and how they operate. This is very much a process of interpretation, during which the participants move freely back and forth across the goals, the resources, and the technical relations that bind them together. The bureaucratic regulations emerge by freezing this ongoing process of interpretation at a particular moment and casting the problem in analytical terms. The goals and the trade-offs among them are clearly specified. The rules are the optimal solution to the analytical problem.

When the regulatory agency where the rules are formulated is sharply distinct from the organizations to which the rules are applied, the latter do not participate in the interpretive process at all. This appears to be the case at the FDA. What we encountered in our case studies was the segment of the regulatory process where the rules were being applied. But the FDA is also engaged in continual discussions—largely with Congress, and through Congress in the broader political arena—about the basic goals of safety and medical efficacy. Regulatory procedures are periodically adjusted to reflect that conversation, just as in product development new products are drawn out of the ongoing interaction between the producer and the customer that preexisting products generate.

The problem for companies that design medical devices is that this broader public discussion does not typically revolve around particular products and therefore seldom encompasses the clinical or patient community. These communities, moreover, are not effectively organized in the way that the industry is organized; their organization seldom is structured to address particular products or treatments. An important exception here, as previously mentioned, is the development of drugs to treat AIDS. In that case, the conversation is both much broader and more specific in terms of the treatments that it addresses, and the process starts to resemble the conversations at the FCC. Perhaps as a consequence, Chiron was able to achieve much more latitude in the way it addressed the clinical community around its viral tests for AIDS than Aspect was able to achieve for BIS.

Regulation in Street-Level Bureaucracies

Bureaucratic rules typically do not operate in a purely mechanical way, and bureaucrats often have some discretion as to how rules are applied. In one important class of bureaucratic agencies, the power actually resides at the base of the bureaucracy and cannot be effectively controlled by rules imposed from above. Michael Lipsky calls these "street-level" bureaucracies.[11]

The classic street level bureaucracy is the police. The rhetoric surrounding police work suggests that the police are charged with enforcing the law. But as James Q. Wilson argues, their task is better understood as maintaining social order. In that endeavor, the law is merely one instrument among many invoked by the officer on the beat to control the situations he encounters—calming the crowd, for example, and removing unmanageable members from the scene. What constitutes "order" in a given situation is ambiguous, continually subject to interpretation by the individual policeman, whose judgment in turn is informed by the ongoing discussions within the police department and between the department and various elements of the community (or communities) whose neighborhoods the police patrol.[12]

Other street-level bureaucrats include the classroom teacher and the welfare case worker. These are typically organizations that have multiple and complex goals, where the relationship between what the line-worker does and the outcomes in terms of any particular goal is complex and not fully understood. In these cases, the interpretive process is ongoing and continuous; it seldom shifts into an overtly analytical mode. Management is about directing a conversation.

A continuing problem in such bureaucracies is that of maintaining consistency of treatment, and hence equity, across different cases. There is no solution to this problem short of forestalling the interpretive process and imposing a set of rigid rules. But the process can be managed through professionalization, where common training and a professional ethos serve to promote consistency. It can also be managed through the creation of specialized units to handle particular types of cases where consistency is important or where the need for discretion is particularly high. Examples are the detective division within the police department, the child welfare division within the welfare department, and the special education division within the school system.

Benchmarking and Merging Horizons

A team of researchers at Columbia Law School, animated by Charles Sabel, has argued that conversations in regulatory agencies can be made more effective by modeling them on the benchmarking process used by many manufacturing firms to force improvements in efficiency.[13] In benchmarking, the company seeks to identify the most efficient practice in the industry for every aspect of its manufacturing process and then judges the performance of its employees by their ability to meet or better the benchmarked standards. In interpretive terms, the benchmarks can be thought of as a means of stimulating, focusing, and directing the conversation.

The Columbia team has been experimenting with benchmarking in a range of regulatory processes, including environmental standards, labor standards, and public education.[14] The idea is to convene the different interests involved in a domain of regulation and then to focus the discussion among those interests, first on the identification of best practice and then on the obstacles to the implementation or replication of that practice in other domains. These procedures thus have the basic properties of the interpretive process as we have characterized it: drawing a group of people from different backgrounds into a sustained conversation and then directing that conversation by selecting the topics around which it will center. The regulator, like the manager in our product development case studies, is no longer the technician solving technical problems, nor is he a mediator negotiating among special interests. He is rather the "hostess" convening and then directing the conversation at the regulatory "cocktail party."

The benchmarking process could of course be understood analytically: the benchmarks could be treated as goals, and the discussion could be focused on the means of achieving them. What makes this process truly interpretive is that the selection of the benchmarks is itself the focal point of the discussion. And the benchmarks can be altered, revised, discarded, or replaced not only in the initial phases of the process but continually, as the discussion about what is really involved in achieving them evolves.

Captive, Cooptation and Corruption

But it is at this point that the dangers of treating regulation as an interpretive process emerge and the fundamental difference between the regulatory arena and other types of public space becomes clear. The difference stems from the fact that interpretation involves a *merging of horizons,* in which people starting from very different places come to share a common understanding. When we translate that into the analytical language of means, ends, and the models that connect them, we are in effect saying either that people starting with different, even conflicting, goals come to share the same goals or—because it is impossible to separate the two positions—they come to share a common sense of the realities that constrain the environment. Possibly both occur. In the interpretive framework, the two are never distinguished. But the problem, when we are talking about regulators and the people they regulate, is, in the analytical language of economics, one of "regulatory capture," or—in layperson's terms—cooptation or even corruption.[15]

Cooptation is a better term than corruption because it conveys an outcome that the people who are actually involved in the process do not themselves perceive. Nevertheless, from the standpoint of the larger public purpose, the process has been compromised. Thus, in the design of a regulatory regime, we must be concerned with a problem that does not arise in the design of other public spaces: how do we insulate the regulators from the effects of the interpretive process?

Intermediary Agencies: The Case of MITRE

The most self-conscious attempt to do this emerged not in our case studies but in an ancillary research project: a study of the internal structure of the MITRE Corporation, a not-for-profit systems engineering company serving clients in various federal government agencies including the Defense Department, the Federal Aviation Administration (FAA), and the Internal Revenue Service (IRS).[16] MITRE is one of a special class of independent organizations, called Federally Funded Research and Development Centers (FFRDCs), created to help the federal government address long-term strategic problems involving complex technologies and systems. By charter, the FFRDCs are prohibited from manufacturing products, competing with private firms, or serving private clients. This is intended to ensure their role as sources of objective, knowledgeable technical advice and counsel. As independent companies, the FFRDCs also have more flexibility than the federal agencies they serve to recruit and retain highly skilled technical personnel.

MITRE became interested in our ideas about interpretation in product development and asked us to examine, from an interpretive perspective, the company's use of information technology and its impact on the corporate organization. We were attracted to the company precisely because it views one of its core missions as mediating between the armed forces, particularly the Air Force, and the civilian economy. In so doing, MITRE enables (or tries to enable) the military to understand and take advantage of developments in civilian industry without diluting its mission of military preparedness.

MITRE's basic organizational problem was to create a separate personality of its own, rather than become either simply a higher-paid extension of the military or an organization guided by commercial incentives as if it were a profit-making firm. Its mission automatically put it at the intersection of two conversations, one with its military interlocutors, the second with the commercial and, to a lesser extent, the academic domains from which the military procures its technologies. Projects were sometimes staffed by two kinds of personnel— those familiar with the emerging technology and those familiar with the particular military problem for which the technology might be a solution. When these two types of expertise fused in particular company personnel, however, MITRE became essentially a pass-through from the commercial to the military world. As a result, there was less of the kind of free-flowing interaction that we have likened to a conversation than there would have been if the military and the commercial worlds were in direct contact. Everybody in this system had become focused on the analytical solution of technical problems.

Thus, the top management at MITRE was concerned with maintaining an internal conversation within the company itself that would substitute for a conversation between the military and the commercial community. It sought to create an independent sense of mission within the company, so that personnel did not simply see themselves as an extension of their military clients. And it created a series of organizational mechanisms to integrate across the domains in which the company worked and to prevent the company from being absorbed into either of the two worlds between which it was supposed to mediate. The organizational mechanisms reflected the range of devices that are discussed in the modern management literature, including matrix management, which operates to limit the immersion of technical experts within their own particular domains, rotation of assignments across domains, the creation within the company of research labs and study groups that cross domains, the development of computer-linked chat groups on particular technologies (for example, Java) that draw people from different departments, and so on.

Once we saw the role that MITRE self-consciously played, we recognized that similar institutions arise in a more spontaneous way in the regulatory arena. In our case studies, this was most apparent at the FDA. The FDA is very concerned about cooptation, but it seems to address that problem, as we have already noted, by holding itself aloof from the commercial organizations that it regulates. This posture is reinforced by the history of spectacular cases of medical failure, such as thalidomide in the early 1960s and Fen-Phen in the late 1990s. But in the face of the organization's own isolation, what has emerged is a layer of intermediaries in the form of lawyers and consultants who advise the companies that must seek FDA approval for their products. The consultants are typically ex-FDA employees who have spent the greater part of their careers with the agency, managing the approval process themselves.

The difference between this group of people and MITRE is that they deliberately function as silos, or pass-throughs, essentially translating the regulations of the FDA and interpreting its ethos for their clients, but not in any way animating an ongoing conversation. Indeed, their existence in some sense forestalls such a conversation. It is possible to imagine various ways in which the FDA could turn this community of consultants into an organization that functions in a manner similar to MITRE—for example, through the sponsoring of research labs or the promotion of continuing (rather than episodic) seminars.

Regulation as Public Space

Regulation has been a central focus of the debate about the competitiveness of the American economy over the last thirty years. Politicians, business leaders, consumer advocates, environmentalists, economists, and others have all weighed in vigorously, and an enormous literature surrounds the subject.

But the ongoing debate about regulation has been conceived almost exclusively in analytical terms. It presupposes a sharp separation between goals and means. The central idea is that regulation is required when the goals of the larger society and the goals of commercial firms diverge. In a properly functioning market, the price system should indicate to the firm both the value of particular outcomes (products, services) and the cost of alternative means of achieving (producing) them. When the market performs this function efficiently, the decisions of the firm will be those that maximize the welfare of society. But if the outcomes are not properly valued—for example, if there are side effects, such as environmental damage, or harm to worker health, or adverse reactions to drugs—that are undervalued in the marketplace, then the optimal outcomes for firm and society will not align. The role of regulation is to prevent this from happening by compensating for market failures.

The most common criticism of the regulatory process is that it is too rigid. It leads to blanket prohibitions when the issues are ones of degree and when they vary with particular circumstances, or it forces firms to respond to a problem in a particular way when the same benefit could be achieved at lower cost by responding in another way. The great countering fear is that any attempt to make regulation more flexible will open the door to distortions of judgment or outright corruption and will allow the commercial interests at stake to overwhelm other values.

The interpretive picture of regulation as the product of a continuous, ongoing conversation relieves much of the rigidity that is the target of the standard criticism. But the ambiguous character of the regulations that would result from this process could create uncertainty and make the regulations difficult to enforce in a consistent and equitable manner. Turning the regulatory arena into a public, conversational space could open the door to distortions by powerful actors who control critical resources or who are attached to a narrow set of values. It is just this kind of imbalance of power that leads to market failure and to the case for regulation in the first place.

The analytical approach guards against these systemic failures, but what it leaves out are the effects of change: technical change on the constraints within which the regulatory process operates, and social change in the weight given to the values that produced the regulations in the first place. These two evolutionary processes—in technology and in social values—interact with each other. The R&D that changes the technical relationships among the constraints is itself partly a response to the social values that produce the regulations; and conversely those values are influenced by the technical possibilities. This interplay between goals and means is continuous; it is what the interpretive process is all about.

And so once again we are faced with the fact that the conversations that underlie the interpretive process cannot be reduced to analytical terms. The problem is exactly analogous to that faced in product development itself: how to manage both processes simultaneously.

UNIVERSITIES AS PUBLIC SPACES

7

The American system of higher education—and within it the research university system—is widely recognized as the nation's central institution for the generation and dissemination of knowledge. The American research university is also generally perceived as an open institution which, in a broad sense, is accessible to society as a whole. This perception was shared by the respondents in our industry case studies, and it was largely responsible for their willingness to participate in our interviews, to give generously of their time, and to respond openly to our questions. The high regard for American research universities was shared by foreign participants as well. Indeed, the U.S. system of higher education and research is viewed in all of the countries we visited as a model to emulate in redesigning their own systems of higher education.[1]

But the particular features of the American research university system that influence its role in the U.S. economy and make it such a powerful engine of technological development are not well understood. The mysteries that surround the universities pose a major problem for public policy. It is a problem for foreign countries wishing to adapt the U.S. model to their own circumstances without necessarily reproducing its every feature. It is also a problem in the United States itself, because the environment in which the universities operate is changing, generating pressures that are propelling them into the commercial arena.

A major pressure is financial. Government support for research and development, which funded much of the post–World War II expansion of the research university system, is no longer a reliable resource. In fields other than the life sciences, the flow of federal research dollars has actually declined in real terms in recent years, even as the number of academic departments and laboratories with the qualifications to compete credibly for these funds has continued to rise. Tuition fees, which might once have been an alternative source of revenue, are no longer a viable substitute. The cost of higher education is already so prohibitive that most universities cannot realistically expect to increase their income from tuition while remaining committed to merit-based admissions.

Just as the competition among universities for federal research dollars intensified, companies began to look more closely at university laboratories as potential contributors to their product development activities. Over the past decade, industry funding for academic research has been growing faster than any other source, although it still accounts for less than 8 percent of the total.[2] Corporate interest has been stimulated by the growing commercial relevance of university research in such potentially important fields as genomics and proteomics, bioengineering, and nanotechnology, as well as by a general trend away from in-house R&D. Many businesses have been increasing their reliance on external sources of technology as a way to control the risks and costs of research.[3]

As the gap between university laboratories and the marketplace has shrunk, academic administrators, faculty members, and legal departments have become more adept at the commercial exploitation of on-campus research. And at the federal, state, and local level, policymakers have welcomed the prospect of an enhanced role for the research universities as agents of economic development. The result has been a variety of programs and policies designed to encourage new university–industry collaborations and more rapid and efficient technology transfer from universities to business.[4]

A third force driving the university toward commercialization should be mentioned, although it is not the focus of this chapter. The new technologies of distance learning hold out the prospect of financial rewards for the owners of proprietary curricula. Some observers predict that eventually the integrity of the university as a geographic entity and locus of direct interaction between instructor and student will be undermined as new players enter this segment of the higher education market. Tension between administrators and faculty over the ownership of curricular materials is just one of many consequences now being felt as the monetary incentives of distance learning are factored into the academic equation.[5]

In sum, a potent brew of competition, economic opportunity, and financial gain is luring research universities into the commercial marketplace. But even as university campuses open themselves up as never before to important constituencies in industry, the partnership is turning out to be less than perfect, even for universities with a strong tradition of working closely with industry.

One reason is that ties to the operating sectors of the economy are not central to the internal design of the university.

The American research university is structured around two distinct functions, education and scholarly research. In education, there are sharp distinctions between graduate professional education and undergraduate education. The former is closely allied with scholarly research, while the latter is only loosely coupled with it. For the purposes of research, the university is structured around scholarly disciplines. The borders of these disciplines are sharply defined, and careers of faculty members are typically influenced more by their standing among peers within their discipline than by their activities within their own university.

Foreign observers frequently note the close ties between universities and industry in the United States, but in fact the borders between the two domains are well maintained. At an elite research university like MIT, faculty are expected to spend no more than one day a week on outside professional activities, and they are required to report all compensated commercial contacts to the university administration. Faculty do engage in commercial ventures of their own in this allotted time, and sometimes spend sabbaticals consulting within an industry. On occasion they leave the academy for the commercial world permanently. But movement in the other direction, at least at the faculty level, is much rarer.

To those hoping to align the research interests of universities more closely with the commercial interests of industry, the internal academic structure of the university is a frustrating obstacle. To those at the other extreme, the preservation of this disciplinary structure and the academic freedom of inquiry it supports is much more critical to American society than any additional contribution the universities might make to commercial innovation and productivity. Absent from these polar positions is a clear understanding of the role that universities are already playing in the economy, and thus of what might be gained and lost in aligning their activities more closely with those of industry.[6]

Our case studies did not help us directly resolve the puzzle of the economic role that American universities play. It seemed, in fact, to vary enormously across the several industries we studied. Academic research was most prominent in medical devices, where core technologies often came directly from university research and where companies served essentially as bridges between the university and the marketplace. For Chiron, which originated in the Biology Department at the University of California at San Francisco, this bridge formed the essential structure of its business plan. Aspect was also founded by a university researcher, and its core technology was first developed as a university project. In this industry, and in the closely allied pharmaceutical and biotechnology sectors, teaching hospitals are frequently a site for drug and device trials and, because of their capacity to influence professional practice, a key target of marketing strategies.

The other industries we studied had a more arms-length relationship to the university system. In those industries, technological advances originating in university research laboratories tended to arrive through intermediaries such as company labs, business consultants, and newly hired university graduates. Joel Spira at Lutron had been quite involved in university governance as an advisor and an active financial donor and had drawn upon many faculty directly as consultants. But Lutron recognized that once Spira retired it would probably rely more heavily on independent consultants who had no direct ties to the university system. Most of the other companies in our study also seemed to draw on university technology only indirectly. The garment industry, which alone among those we studied did not depend on the system of higher education to staff its design operations, nevertheless saw the university campus as a critical market for its products and the student culture as a vital inspiration for design ideas.

While the cases alone did not resolve the question of the universities' economic role, the conceptual distinction between analysis and interpretation that we drew from them adds an important dimension to the debate. It has led us to see more clearly what is at stake as universities confront the challenges of the marketplace. Not only is the integrity of the academic enterprise itself at risk, as the purists contend; also threatened is the dynamism of the larger system of innovation of which both the universities and industry are *already* a part. In the sections that follow, we will elaborate on the fragile nature of this economic ecosystem and its vulnerability to the pressures of commercialization.

Interpretation and Public Space

As we have seen, research and new product development can occur in two different kinds of "spaces": commercial (proprietary) and public. In the United States the university is unquestionably the most important public space for research and development.

University research, like industrial R&D, can be either analytical or interpretive in character. The dual nature of university R&D was illustrated in a recent book by Rosalind Williams, in which she reflected on her experiences as dean of students at MIT. She recalled that when the provost was confronted with a particularly difficult organizational challenge, his confident response ("This is MIT. We're engineers. Engineers solve problems.") captured for many faculty members the essence of their community. But later in the book Williams offers a very different summation of the ethos at MIT, this one drawn from her participation on a faculty committee convened to examine the quality of student life:

> Over two years of study, we concluded that MIT has been so fertile in technological creativity—so innovative, if you will—because of informal groups, unstructured encounters, odd connections, wandering, and daydreaming. MIT's common resources gave us time and space to graze . . . In a quite hard-headed way, we argued that the sources of creativity necessary to engender change, technological or otherwise, flourish only in a setting with time and space for the intense social interactions that are at the heart of both research and learning.[7]

It is a safe bet that many of those for whom MIT is quintessentially about problem solving would also have no difficulty recognizing their university in Williams's interpretive description.[8]

Firms that draw on university research and development certainly seem aware of both the analytical and interpretive dimensions of campus research, even if they do not use those terms to describe them. One recent study which examined twenty-one university research centers and nearly two hundred collaborating firms found that for some firms the main goal was to enlist university researchers in problem-solving activities directly related to their primary business. In these interactions, the impact on the company's bottom line was the dominant measure of performance. But for other firms, the most important objectives of their interactions with the university were to participate in activities and exchanges that would enable them to become privy to the latest thinking in fields relevant to their business, and also to have an influence on the future direction of related curricula at the university.[9]

In general, firms in this second category tended to be larger, and the universities with whom they collaborated tended to be those in the elite group. The more problem-focused collaborations were more likely to involve small and medium-sized firms and lower-ranked universities. Another study found that firms are about as likely to use research from universities and other public research laboratories to suggest ideas for new R&D projects as they are to use it to help them complete existing projects.[10] Again, this suggests an awareness among firms of the dual character of university research.

Although the analytical–interpretive duality is present in universities just as it is in firms, important differences between the two settings complicate relations between the two entities. Yet these differences are viewed positively by many firms. University researchers have incentives to pick out problems for analytical solution that are generally not the same as those that their counterparts in firms would choose. Corporate researchers are motivated by economic goals. They choose problems whose solution is expected to lead to commercially attractive new products and processes or to the improvement of existing ones. University researchers are more likely to be influenced by other considerations, although exactly what these considerations are is not always easy to articulate. It is often said that what differentiates a great university researcher from a very good one is not so much the ability to solve problems as the ability to figure out which problems are most important to address. The implication is that identifying such problems is in some sense a mysterious, intuitive process.

Be that as it may, the scholarly disciplines clearly exert a powerful influence on problem identification. At any given moment one can usually recognize a prevailing view within a discipline concerning the areas in which new knowledge is most needed, which problems are most important to address, and indeed which problems *can* be addressed with the scientific methods available to that discipline. That is not to say that the voice of the discipline is the only one to which university researchers listen. In many cases they are also motivated by a practical purpose—finding a cure for multiple sclerosis, alleviating unemployment, defending against a security threat, or developing a renewable source of energy. But without doubt, the scholarly disciplines play a much larger role in the selection of problems for analytical solution in universities than in firms.

It is also true that the practical purposes which influence problem selection in the university are more likely to be *public* purposes—that is, socially important purposes that are not readily valued by the market and for which the market mechanism is therefore not optimal for achieving the ultimate result. In commercial firms, by contrast, financial gain is almost always the primary practical motivation. Social gains are secondary and may be undermined by the firm's primary objective. The long-term social costs of gas-guzzling cars, processed foods, expensive drugs, coal-burning factories, pesticide run-off, destruction of the ozone shield, and other undesirable consequences of economic activity are not readily factored into an individual company's bottom line, unless regulation has forced them there.

Just as analytical problem solving differs between universities and firms, so too does the interpretive process. In both settings the conversations that underlie the interpretive process have a direction, but in commercial firms it primarily addresses commercial interests. In the university, the conversation is directed toward advancing the frontier of discovery or toward a particular public purpose.

These differences between firms and universities are clarified by a map of research and development drawn by Donald Stokes.[11] He invented his map as an alternative to what had long been the prevailing view of R&D—that it could be separated into basic or fundamental research, on the one hand, and applied research and development on the other. In this conventional view, basic research provides a vital reservoir of knowledge on which development draws, but it should be conducted essentially independently of it. Stokes pointed out that research can be, and very often is, simultaneously motivated by the challenge of advancing the frontier of fundamental knowledge *and* by a desire to achieve some practical goal. The conventional schemata implied that these motivations were mutually exclusive.

In Stokes's framework, research—or, at least, the motivations of researchers—can be diagrammed by a simple two-by-two matrix. The upper left-hand cell describes research

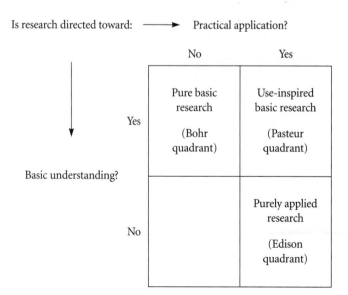

that is being pursued for its own sake, without thought of practical application and with the sole objective of pushing forward the frontier of scientific understanding. Stokes called this the Bohr quadrant, in reference to the fundamental studies of atomic structure conducted by the Danish physicist Niels Bohr early in the twentieth century.

The lower right quadrant refers to work that is solely motivated by practical objectives. For Stokes the archetypal practitioner of this kind of work was Thomas Edison. In his laboratory, existing knowledge was deployed in the service of practical applications, but Edison actively discouraged his researchers from exploring the deeper scientific implications of their discoveries.

The upper-right cell describes research that is both fundamental in character and motivated by practical concerns. Stokes referred to this as Pasteur's quadrant, after the great nineteenth-century French scientist. His very practical goals of preventing the spoilage of milk and other foods and treating diseases in humans and animals led him to undertake fundamental investigations in microbiology. The modern field of genomics provides many examples of Pasteur-type research today. It is difficult to imagine anything more fundamental than the study of biology at the cellular and molecular levels. But much of this research is also motivated by the very practical objectives of discovering the mechanisms of particular diseases and developing effective therapies for them, as well as, for some researchers, the prospect of financial reward.

The lower left-hand quadrant refers to research that has neither a practical purpose nor any aspiration to advance the frontier of scientific understanding. Occasionally its practitioners stumble across a great insight, but their more mundane purpose is usually to fill in small gaps of knowledge within an already mature field. There are many examples of this work—Stokes cited the taxonomic studies of the naturalist Roger Tory Peterson—but this category is not relevant for our purposes here.

The work carried out by corporate research and development organizations spans all three active quadrants of Stokes's matrix, but much of what is done—and certainly almost everything under the heading of product development—falls within the Edison quadrant. University research also spans all three cells, though most of its activity tends to concentrate in the Bohr and Pasteur quadrants.

Researchers operating in each quadrant are engaged in both analytical and interpretive activities. Problem solving occurs everywhere, as does open-ended conversation. But the character of those conversations depends both on where they occur on Stokes's map and on whether they take place in universities or in firms. For research in Pasteur's quadrant, the conversations are influenced both by the relevant scientific disciplines and by practical purposes. In firms, however, those practical purposes always include commercial gain, whereas in universities other purposes are more likely to give the conversation its sense of direction.

Another way in which interpretive processes within the university differ from those in firms is in their diversity and openness to new participants. The university is a focus of conversation and debate that extends beyond the disciplines and, often, beyond the walls of the campus itself. Some of these conversations center on the curriculum. Both undergraduate programs and professional graduate schools draw on multiple disciplines, and the development and administration of these programs entails ongoing interactions among disciplinary specialists. These often involve the kind of academic infighting and turf wars for which universities are notorious, but they also engage a broad chorus of voices in substantive debate about what constitutes an appropriate education and about how concepts and ideas from different disciplines can be combined in order to provide that education most effectively.

The capacity to create new interdisciplinary research programs and laboratories is another way in which new participants are drawn into the interpretive conversations on campus. Such units at American universities are still relatively rare—rare enough so that the procedures governing them are not well established. But in recent years they have become a good deal more common, and the new interdisciplinary laboratories often play an important role in sheltering the early stages of conversation about new technical domains. At MIT, the Research Laboratory for Electronics, the Laboratory for Computer Science, and the Media Laboratory are among the best-known of more than thirty such interdisciplinary centers and institutes.[12]

Conversations about research and education on university campuses are also open to faculty and students from around the world, as well as to external participants, including industrialists. Indeed, the research universities are among the most internationalized institutions in American society.[13] And the complex financial and governance structure of American universities draws people from a variety of sectors and backgrounds into close and continuing contact with the university and its ongoing operations. This includes business and government as institutional actors, but it also includes university alumni, who are typically spread throughout society and across the globe.

The ability of the disciplines to restrict and sometimes confound these conversations should not be underestimated, and we will return to remedies shortly. Still, the conversations about education and research on university campuses involve a much more diverse and unpredictable set of participants than is typically found within a commercial enterprise and are generally also more open to new interlocutors. A university functions as a kind of public forum in a way that firms cannot.

The value of these differences is recognized by at least some of those in industry who now look to the universities to play a greater role in their product development activities. It is not just the availability of highly skilled specialists and state-of-the-art facilities that attracts industrialists. In fact, the high indirect cost rate applied to university research means that it is often not cost-competitive with either for-profit or other kinds of nonprofit research organizations. What mainly attracts product developers to university campuses is the opportunity to participate in interpretive conversations that are different in direction and broader in scope and participation than those within firms.

And here lies the problem. Many of the proposals for opening up university research more fully to the needs of such firms would diminish these very differences. The most far-reaching proposals would make the university, in effect, the R&D arm of industry. But even more modest proposals would link the analytical problem solving that takes place in the universities more closely to industrial needs. The range of possibilities being discussed was described by a senior industrial research director during a university seminar:

> Can you in universities consider getting closer to the strategic needs of companies? This means being aware of key plans to gain competitive advantage, or involvement in producing the wish list of technological breakthroughs that companies might need for the longer term. It could also mean having students under your

guidance that might work on these areas for a company and not be allowed to publish until patents are secured, or possibly even delaying publication for very long times if ever. Can you conceive of forming special alliances with companies that promise exclusivity for the deliverables for extended periods of time? Can you imagine having your professors spend part of their time working for the specific interests of private companies, and counting this favorably towards their promotions and tenure ratings? Can you imagine having your students doing doctoral work under professors but in the labs of companies?[14]

Universities are indeed imagining such things, and many are acting on them. The likely consequences, however, are three-fold. One is that the mix of analytical problems being worked on in the university will more closely mirror the problems being worked on in business. Second, to the degree that analytical problem solving feeds into the ongoing conversations in the university (and the problems that researchers are working on are, after all, what they tend to talk about with their colleagues), the interpretive process within the university will tend to converge with that in industry as well. Third, conversations on campus will become less open. Analytical problem solving that is relevant to business has commercial value by definition. This creates incentives for faculty to shelter their research from their colleagues so that they can take it to market themselves. It also sets off a competition between the university and its own faculty for proprietary rights, again increasing the risk that certain members of the faculty will withdraw from the conversation altogether. And the attempts of industry sponsors to secure the broadest possible rights to intellectual property generated on campus will, if unchecked, similarly constrain the conversation.

Debate about these changes has centered on the perceived risks to the university as an institution—the threats to academic collegiality, to the openness of communication among faculty and between faculty and students, to the integrity of research results, to the freedom that faculty have to pursue research interests without interference, and so on. The analytical–interpretive framework highlights another risk: that such changes, while making the universities more responsive to industry, may also jeopardize what at least some firms see as the most valuable contribution the universities can make to business innovation: the interpretive activity on campus. Too close an alliance between industry and academia threatens to make both interpretive conversation and its analytical counterpart not much different from what already takes place in firms.

Disciplines and Interdisciplines

In sounding this warning against the commercialization of university research, we do not mean to idealize the current university environment. On the contrary, our notion of the role of public space in the development of new products and services also points quite clearly to the limitations of the discipline-based structure of the universities and the importance of overcoming them.

The organization of knowledge into disciplines and subdisciplinary specialties has of course been crucial to scientific progress. The advances of the past fifty years would have been inconceivable without these "silos," given the vast scope of the modern scientific enterprise and the difficulties confronting individual researchers seeking to keep up with more than

a very small fraction of the whole. But the disciplinary structure of the universities is a serious barrier to the kinds of
cross-border conversations that we have argued are critical to
product innovation and to the preservation of the public
spaces that are needed for its pursuit. The kinds of uninhib-
ited conversational exchanges that qualify the university as a
public space tend not to occur across the boundaries of disciplines. If anything, the structure of the university discourages
such border crossing. The primary contribution of the university has been the conversations that occur *within* disciplinary boundaries.

Even within the disciplines, the competition for recognition creates incentives for scholars to hide what they are doing from one another. In this sense, competition within the
university appears to resemble the rivalry that occurs between firms. But this is not really a very good analogy. Though
often intensely competitive with one another, scholars also
draw heavily on their colleagues' work, and few scholarly contributions are possible without participation in the larger discourse. Competitive pressure thus also creates a counterin-
centive to secrecy—a need to talk about one's research with
other scholars so that one's ideas can advance.

How these contradictory pressures operate is often difficult for nonpractitioners to understand. A very revealing
description is provided in James D. Watson's autobiographi-
cal account of the discovery of the structure of DNA, *The
Double Helix*.[15] Watson discusses at some length the relationships that he and Francis Crick had with other researchers
whose work made their own discoveries possible but who
were also in a race with them to be the first to identify the
molecular structure of DNA. In an academic research community with a shared commitment to intellectual pursuit as a

primary goal, there is a sort of ethic of gift exchange, but that ethic is managed deliberately with the practical goal of keeping vital information flowing.

Ultimately, what seems most important in countervailing the incentives for secrecy in academic research is the nature of the disciplines as communities of identity. The members' sense of themselves and their value as individuals is rooted in their discipline, and they look to their colleagues for recognition and reaffirmation. In a sense, colleagues working in the same field are the only people able truly to appreciate the value of a scholar's endeavor. And the greatest accomplishment is to have a colleague pick up one's research and build upon it in his own. To achieve this kind of recognition, one must reveal the results of one's work and have it freely examined by others and widely discussed. An important feature of scholarship is, therefore, that ideas, once formulated, are made public and enter permanently into the public domain and discourse; secrecy is confined to the process of discovery.

The role played by the disciplines in the interpretive processes occurring in the university is thus complex and in some sense contradictory. On the one hand, the disciplinary communities provide the setting for the great majority of the ongoing conversations on campus having to do with the creation of new knowledge, as well as the motivation and the direction for these conversations. On the other hand, the boundaries these communities draw around themselves inhibit the kinds of cross-disciplinary discussions that are so important for new product development.

Managing, not Muddying, the University's Borders

Just as with business firms, so it is with universities: in thinking about them we tend to be prisoners of the analytical perspective. We need not, and cannot, abandon that view, but it should be augmented with an interpretive perspective, to both temper and complement the analytical approach.

On university campuses, as in firms, interpretive conversations occur alongside problem solving. And just as in firms, the participants in these conversational exchanges draw out of them specific problems whose analytical solution brings benefits to the problem solvers and to society more generally. But the on-campus variants of both interpretive and analytical processes differ from their counterparts in the business sector.

Faculty members compete with one another within disciplinary communities but also depend on these communities for recognition and reputation. Because individuals rely on their competitors to judge and appreciate their accomplishments, and because they are dependent as well upon their colleagues' discoveries to develop their own, the competitive incentive to hide one's work is tempered by the need to reveal it and share it. The result is an ethos of openness. As universities compete with one another for faculty drawn from these disciplinary communities, this ethos of openness is projected onto the university system as a whole.

Whereas analytical activity in business is generally motivated by profit, in the university it is typically driven by the desire for recognition within the disciplinary community or the desire to contribute to some public good. The interpretive process on campus is also different. To a much greater degree than in business firms, the disciplines dominate the conversations; but the diversity of perspectives is greater than in firms because academic discussions draw in a broader range of participants, and withdrawal from the conversation on proprietary grounds is the exception rather than the rule. Even accounting for the restrictive influence of the disciplines, a university, far more than a firm, is a public space.

The first important conclusion of this chapter, then, is the need to maintain this diversity and openness. The second has to do with merging horizons in the interpretive process. In any conversation, diversity among participants tends to decline over time, as they develop a common language through their interaction. In a sense, the development of such a common language is the outcome desired. And the university does periodically spin off new communities of practice in the form of new academic disciplines or new fields of commercial endeavor. But the integrity of the larger process requires that the basic participants preserve their separate identities— that they retain their roots in the independent conversations that create and shape these identities.

The involvement of businesspeople, with their commercial interests and incentives, adds a unique perspective to the conversations on campus. But if the interests of business are fully assimilated by the university participants—that is, if there is a complete merging of horizons—not only will something be lost from the conversation, but the value to industry itself will be diminished. If MIT researchers start thinking like Microsoft researchers, the university will no longer be able to add anything to Microsoft's own interpretation of the world. Its view will no longer be distinctive.

The analytical–interpretive duality does not allow us to say exactly what the optimal level of industry involvement on campus should be. It certainly does not lead to the conclusion that business practitioners ought to be excluded from academic discourse, or that any analytical activity on campus that is directed toward commercial goals should be avoided. But it does point to the need for limits on university behavior.

The private, proprietary arrangements that some universities are cultivating with particular business firms look particularly suspicious in this regard, for several reasons.

First, they undermine the universities' reputation as a public space and thus their ability to draw on other funds, particularly government funds and the donations of private individuals; and they weaken the ties that these other funding arrangements create between the university and other operating sectors. They are also likely to draw faculty members away from their disciplinary commitments and to undermine their ability to build scholarly reputations and to draw on the research results of their colleagues, who, when they find results being withheld, are likely to withhold their own results in response. Such a development would in the long run threaten the whole ethos of openness within the system. Of course, it may also be self-correcting, in the sense that exclusive arrangements between the university and industry are likely to weaken the ability of the institutions that initiate such agreements to attract top scholars.

Over the past two decades universities have adopted a wide variety of ways to organize their relations with industry, including technology licensing operations, for-profit research affiliates, incubation space for new spin-off companies, industrial liaison programs, industry-wide research consortia, large-scale relationships with individual corporations, interdisciplinary research centers focused on the needs of particular industries, on-campus "embedded" corporate laboratories, and internal regulations governing conflict of interest and commitment. More research on the effectiveness of these arrangements is needed.

But industry itself has already delivered a verdict on one such approach. A proposal at MIT to create a "halfway house" —a facility for joint university–industry research that would be physically adjacent to the campus and thus convenient for university research staff but administratively distinct from the university and free of its restrictions on proprietary research—was emphatically rejected by a group of senior industrialists to whom it was recently presented. They made clear that what was most important to them was the opportunity to locate their researchers on the MIT campus itself. They saw greater value in participating in the open, interpretive processes on campus than in engaging the university researchers in the proprietary problem solving that the off-campus setting would permit.

LEARNING THE RIGHT LESSONS ABOUT COMPETITIVENESS

8

We return finally to the questions with which this book began. How do we explain America's resurgence as the dominant power in the global economy during the 1990s? What are the right lessons to draw from that period for the future? What must be done next in order to sustain the competitiveness of the American economy?

On the central question of innovation, we argue that the lessons learned up to this point are, if not outright wrong, then seriously deficient. Those lessons emphasize the effectiveness of market forces in inducing innovation, while essentially ignoring the interpretive processes that are the wellspring of creativity in the economy. The dominant approach to innovation seeks to strengthen and extend the domain of market competition. But the interpretive perspective points in the opposite direction, toward the creation of sheltered spaces that can sustain public conversation among a diversity of economic actors who would be unable to interact in this way on their own. Unless a better balance is established in both management strategies and policy priorities, we face a real danger that the nation's innovative performance, so vital for its prosperity in the long run, will flag.

How Did We Get to This Point?

In the 1980s, the debate about America's economic competitiveness focused on manufacturing cost and quality—domains where the United States was in danger of falling behind Japan and other advanced economies. Since that time, the emphasis has shifted to innovation, where the United States is the recognized leader and where the central question is how to strengthen our innovative capabilities further. As huge pools of low-cost labor in China, India, and other developing nations merge with the global economy, expert opinion in the United States has embraced an economic model that emphasizes innovation. Almost everyone agrees that a technologically dynamic domestic economy, prolific in the invention and application of new products and services, is the only path to sustainable prosperity. As one government official recently observed, "America must never compete in the battle to see who can pay their workers least, and it will take sustained innovation to ensure that we don't have to."[1]

In tandem with this move toward innovation, both public policy and business practices have also shifted, toward heavier emphasis on markets in creating an environment where innovation can flourish. Fifteen years ago or even ten, the view of markets in the economic debate was more complex. One influential diagnosis blamed the flagging competitiveness of large, vertically integrated American companies on their isolation from market pressures. The solution was both to expose these companies to more intense competition and to expand the reach of market incentives into the firm itself—through increased use of individual bonuses, merit raises, and stock options. But an alternative diagnosis blamed competitiveness problems on structural weaknesses within American industry, especially in comparison with its Japanese and German competitors. The problem was a lack of integration and flexibility—an inability to overcome obstacles to cooperation and coordination between companies and their suppliers, between different components of the firm, and between management and labor.

According to this second opinion, the surgical corrective for these traditional vertically-integrated firms, with their clean functional divisions and clear lines of authority, was to flatten the hierarchy, decentralize decision-making, and pump up cross-functional teams and network organizations. Different parts of the firm were empowered to work with one another and with outside collaborators without constant resort to supervisors higher up the chain of command. Many of the particular techniques and processes were borrowed from Japanese industry, including Total Quality Management, lean production, the *kanban* system, and concurrent engineering, sometimes with adaptations to fit the American workplace. The goal was to create nimble organizations, capable of responding quickly and efficiently to rapidly changing market conditions.

These two prescriptions—more competition, more coordination and integration—were contradictory in their view of the market. While the former sought to extend the influence of market incentives, the latter encouraged collaborations of the very sort that marketplace competition could be expected to inhibit. But most people seemed not to be bothered by this inconsistency—or even to be aware of it (partly because the two prescriptions were advocated by two different sets of people).

Beginning in the 1990s, the balance between the two prescriptions began to shift, as small entrepreneurial firms, many of them venture-financed, made their mark with a host of innovative products and services in information technology, biotechnology, and many other sectors. Around the same time, the Japanese and German economies—models of integration for many in American industry in earlier years—faltered, and the competitive threat from their industries diminished. The contrasts grew sharper as the decade wore on. The U.S. economy, whose policy gurus were enthusiastic about deregulation and the rigors of the marketplace, continued its powerful expansion, while in Japan and much of Europe, where such enthusiasm was considerably less wholehearted, economic growth stagnated and innovation in cutting-edge industries lagged well behind the dynamic performance of the American high-technology sector.

As the United States has struggled to absorb the economic setbacks of the new decade and to understand the successes of the 1990s, the interest in organizational restructuring has continued to wane, while the strategic importance of market incentives is emphasized more than ever. Economic policymakers as well as industrialists in the private sector have embraced the idea that the key to an innovative economy is to ensure that prospective innovators are exposed to the right set of market incentives. Consequently, policymakers see as their most crucial task establishing, enforcing, and maintaining such an incentive system. Similarly, American business leaders have increasingly sought to harness market incentives in their innovation efforts. They see as *their* most important task clearing the decks in the firm so that competition can do its work, outsourcing activities—including even new product development—if it is more efficient to do so, and aligning internal incentives with those of the firm's stockholders as closely as possible.

Increased competitive pressures generated by globalization, technological change, and deregulation have certainly helped to raise the efficiency of the U.S. economy over the past decade. But their role in stimulating innovation is not nearly as clear. As these pressures have built, in fact, the space for interpretive processes in the economy has narrowed. And the push to extend the reach of market incentives is further eroding this space. The lessons drawn from the boom of the 1990s have overlooked the contribution of interpretive processes to innovation and economic growth. Despite the enormous strength of America's technological assets and capabilities, the current thrust of policy and practice raises real questions about whether our economy's innovative performance can be sustained.

Analysis and Interpretation in Product Development

Our strong views on these issues grow out of our findings on the nature of product design and development in a limited number of fields. This is a narrow base from which to address such broad questions, and we begin by restating exactly what those findings are. Our core finding is the fundamental distinction between analysis and interpretation as two complementary approaches to design and development. The analytical approach, which dominates industrial management and engineering practice, is essentially problem solving and rational choice as these skills are taught in business and technology schools and as understood conceptually in economics and the allied social sciences.

Interpretive processes, by contrast, are akin to conversations, and the manager's activities mirror those of the hostess at a cocktail party. The "interpretive" manager draws the critical actors together, encourages them to talk to one another, and introduces new members or new topics to the group when conversation lags. What emerges from these conversations is a language community within which new products are conceived and discussed. Interpretive processes therefore evolve in the same way that new languages develop over time, or in the way that new members are drawn into an existing language community. In both cases, one learns to "speak the language" to the point where it is possible to distinguish between genuine ambiguity and simple confusion. This linguistic capability can then be used to explore ambiguities for the new interpretations they can generate, which in turn lead to product innovation.

Analysis and interpretation are not only distinct, they are in many ways contradictory and antagonistic to each other. Analysis is organized around projects; it strives for clarity and closure. Interpretation is not a project but a process, ongoing in time, open-ended. It operates in the space created by ambiguity—a space that analysis seeks to close up and ultimately eliminate. Interpretation and analysis are so different, and yet so mutually essential, that we have come to think of them as analogous to the wave and particle theories of light in physics. Each is necessary for successful product development, and innovation cannot be fully understood without reference to both. But at any given moment an individual has to choose one lens or the other; innovation cannot be viewed in both ways at the same time.

Ultimately, analysis prevails: a particular design must be chosen and its properties optimized so that it can be produced efficiently and marketed at a profitable price. But at each moment, the range of alternative design possibilities available for consideration is determined by the ongoing interpretive process. A firm's capacity to engage in both of these contradictory activities simultaneously and to find a balance between them over time is central to successful product development; and on a larger scale it is the key to an innovative economy.

Achieving this dual capacity is difficult in the marketplace because the pressures of competition encourage opportunism and create an atmosphere in which differences of interpretation are easily mistaken for self-interested attempts to gain advantage through manipulation and deception. Interpretive processes are particularly vulnerable to these pressures in the early stages of product development, before a rich language for exploring ambiguity has fully developed. At that early stage, genuine ambiguity is not easily isolated from simple confusion and misunderstanding, and the conversation is fragile and easily abandoned. Especially in its nascent stages, therefore, interpretation needs to be protected from the pressures of competition. It needs a sheltered space where a shared language can develop, where the risk of private appropriation of information is reduced, where actions are less likely to be misunderstood, and where misunderstandings have fewer direct consequences.

What do these findings mean for the broader policy debate about America's economic competitiveness? Our central contention is that spaces for interpretation have grown steadily narrower over the past two decades, as competitive pressures in the U.S. economy have increased. In the immediate postwar decades such protected spaces were fairly widespread. They existed not just in the public and nonprofit domains but in the profit-making sector itself, where large corporate businesses and industrial districts of small firms were able to build shelters inside their boundaries in which interpretive communities could thrive.

The competition unleashed by globalization, technological change, and deregulation has reduced the scope for conversation and interpretation in private industry. This in turn has created a need to expand such spaces outside industry itself, in sectors of society where competitive pressures do not naturally reach. The trouble is that exactly the opposite lesson has been drawn. Convinced that it was the competitive pressures *themselves* that were ultimately responsible for the boom of the 1990s, policymakers and business lobbyists have sought to reproduce in public spaces unconstrained by the market precisely the kinds of competitive mechanisms that are imposed on private business by market forces.

If we are right in our view, the ability of the U.S. economy to sustain the kinds of innovation that helped drive the growth of the 1990s must now be called into question. It is important to remember that the critical early stages of the interpretive process that made those innovations possible actually took place much earlier, during the 1980s and 1970s, and in some cases earlier still. But the institutions that nurtured and encouraged those early conversations are now being fundamentally revised and reoriented in response to the supposed lessons of America's success. Some of them have already been dismantled.

We cannot verify this claim fully on the basis of the small number of case studies presented in this book. Rigorous proof would require an inventory of the innovations that were most important to the expansion of the last decade and the developmental processes that preceded them. But there is certainly no shortage of evidence in our cases to support this claim.

Take cellular technology, for example, which emerged in the shelter of AT&T's Bell Laboratories during the 1960s and 1970s. Although those laboratories still exist, in the midst of the boom they were almost completely transformed—and their sheltering properties eliminated—by deregulation and the resulting breakup of AT&T. In other telecommunication firms we studied, early development of cell phones was financed by taxing the traditional activities of a large, diverse conglomerate. Today, some of the industry's most prominent companies, such as Motorola and Nokia, have shed many of those other activities and are no longer in a position to support the kinds of long-term development processes that sustained the early cellular industry.

Among the major actors in the technological revolution of the 1990s were bioengineering and biotechnology firms, and the new medical devices that we studied were representative of this sector. Like so many biotechnical innovations, Chiron's DNA-based diagnostic techniques and Aspect's BIS index grew out of basic research in university departments—public spaces that are now at the center of the debate about intellectual property ownership. Academic departments are evolving in ways that make them more responsive to the marketplace, and many people see advantages in closer collaborations with business interests. But as a result, the university is in danger of becoming much less congenial to the free-flowing interpretive conversation which is its main strength.

Another wellspring of innovation during the 1990s, the Internet, enjoyed the support of the defense budget during its early years and the protection of university and government R&D laboratories. Funded by the DoD's Advanced Research Projects Agency, it began as the ARPAnet—a computer network created in the late 1960s to allow computers at research facilities across the country to communicate across great distances. The goal was to share resources by handing them off from computer to computer across the net. The Internet has already given birth to an extraordinary range of new businesses, with much more to follow. But the tidal wave of commercialization is encroaching on the space for creative, open conversation that the Internet originally made possible, and proprietary restrictions on the free flow of information across the net are now reaching back into the university departments and research institutes that first harbored it.[2]

The position we are taking here has far-reaching implications, and we do not want to overstate our case. The world is a complicated place, and the complications are important to recognize. A more nuanced view suggests that the situation is both worse and better than the way we have just portrayed it. It is worse because the U.S. economy is developing in directions that make interpretive processes more important than ever to economic progress, even as the available spaces for interpretation appear to be shrinking. It is better because the interpretive perspective also highlights strengths of American society whose competitive potential has not been widely tapped and whose effects have yet to be fully felt.

First the Not-So-Good News

Why is the interpretive approach becoming more critical than ever, even as spaces where these conversations are protected disappear? Several developments are pushing in this direction. One is the decline of mass production as the dominant paradigm for technological development. In the mass production system, even though customers may prefer specially tailored products, the standard product is so much less expensive to produce that it overwhelms more customized alternatives in the marketplace. The cost advantage derives from the economies of scale associated with the use of dedicated tools and machinery and narrowly trained workers. The economic benefit of using these highly specialized resources to produce a single, standardized product creates pressure on the producer to freeze the product design as quickly as possible. The producer has little incentive to continuously reinterpret the world of the consumer, and great incentive to convert both product design and production design into a series of analytical decisions.

But over the past thirty years, as advances in information technology and the techniques of flexible manufacturing have reduced the cost of product variety, the economy has moved progressively away from the mass production model. Through changes in software, production systems can now more easily be adjusted to produce a range of products; they do not need to be physically designed or retooled with a particular product in mind.

An increasingly volatile, unpredictable economic environment, with its "just-in-time" mindset and low inventories, also favors more flexible production arrangements and the technologies that support them. And as the cost of tailoring the product to the needs or tastes of particular consumers or subgroups of consumers has fallen, the premium on interpretive processes that link the product designer to the customer, on one side, and the designer to the production process, on the other, has grown correspondingly. This trend has been further reinforced by the effects of globalization and the movement of what remains of standardized, labor-intensive production to low-wage countries abroad. What is left at home, increasingly, are the kinds of economic activities that are more likely to depend on direct, face-to-face conversation.

Augmenting all these trends has been the blurring of traditional sector boundaries across much of the economy. Previously distinct industries, whose firms virtually never met in the marketplace, now find themselves in direct competition with one another. A striking example is the interpenetration of telecommunications, information technology, office equipment, and photography. IBM, Kodak, and Xerox now compete head-to-head, and they all battle for market share with AT&T and the various telecommunication companies that grew out of it in the course of deregulation. These companies, in turn, spar with the cellular companies and, at the margin (although threatening at any moment to become central to the industry), with Microsoft and other software producers, and even with producers of chips and other hardware components like Intel. And in a different direction, all of these companies now find themselves pulled into the entertainment and media industries, as "content" is repackaged for multimedia outlets. As the old industry boundaries have dissolved, the companies find themselves compelled to learn to talk to one another and to create a shared language.

Last, and underlying all these other developments, is the growing importance of software to economic development. Software is at once emblematic of the change in the organization of the economy and a major component of it. Software development now accounts for a large and increasing proportion of product development in a wide range of industries, even those closely identified with hardware products. At Lutron, the lighting controls firm, for example, software absorbs 55 percent of the development budget. Software is emblematic because it defies the model of the division of labor that lies at the heart of mass production and the analytical approach to product design.

From the very beginning, as we have seen, people have tried to organize software development by breaking projects into separate, discrete components and assigning them to different programmers or programming teams. But it has proved impossible, on a systematic basis, to identify components that have this separable property. When projects are organized this way and the components are put back together, the pieces invariably interact with one another in complex and unpredictable ways to produce bugs. In extreme cases, these incompatibilities bring down the whole system and require hours of skilled programming to find and resolve.

Our case studies suggest why this is the case. The production of software is basically a design process. (The actual "manufacture" of a software program is trivial; almost anyone can do it by inserting a diskette into a personal computer.) As with any design process, the problems of integration are minimized whenever the pieces into which the product is divided are independent of each other. Separability is the goal, and approaches to the problem of achieving it with some degree of regularity and predictability have dominated the literature on software development since its inception. The latest approach is object-oriented programming.[3] The objects are separable components that are independent of each other, so that adjustments can be made within each object without affecting the other parts of the program. But the desired objects are like the two ends of Nam Suh's canonical church key opener: their properties are easy to specify, but finding objects that actually have these properties in any particular case is more of an art than a science.

Imagine breaking up the design of a shirt into subtasks and assigning each component to a separate designer—the right sleeve to one designer, the left sleeve to another, the collar to a third, the front to a fourth, and so on. The problem of integrating these separate designs to form a single, coherent garment is analogous to debugging a software program. The individual components would be bound to clash with one another and would have to be revised when they were put together. In practice, of course, individual garments are never designed this way. But large fashion collections typically are split up among the members of a team, with different garments assigned to different designers. When the collection is brought together at the end, however, it has to be "edited" and many items discarded, just as a software program has to be debugged.

For smaller software programs, companies often use a single architect-programmer-coder for the whole project, who integrates the pieces in his head, imposes his vision on the rest of the team, and checks the work of team members to ensure conformity with it; he is essentially the heavyweight project manager that we saw in automobile design. An alternative approach—and for larger projects the only practical one—is an integrated team that develops a common vision and then works together to ensure that the vision is maintained and the various pieces conform to it as the project evolves.

The importance of having people on the team who share the overall vision leads to the paradox of the "mythical man-month": if a project falls behind schedule and you attempt to catch up by adding staff to the design team at the last minute, the effect is actually to prolong the development period.[4] The problem is that the late arrivals fail to appreciate the overall architecture of the program and how their own work relates to it, and this just increases the number of bugs and delays. A more efficient approach is to grow the development team organically.

The importance of conveying the vision through face-to-face contact also explains the startling fact, revealed in recent studies of offshore software development, that when pieces of programming projects are sent to low-wage countries like India and Mexico for execution, at least 30 percent of the offshore contractor's personnel are located at the client's office in the United States at any given point, and the major managerial task for these projects is to keep this figure from creeping upward over time.[5] It seems clear that a software development project cannot simply be "thrown over the wall," to be implemented by offshore developers.

In the software industry, the intractability of the problem of integration and coordination has led instead to a pattern of organic growth through direct communication in conversation—a canonical example of an interpretive design community.

The Good News

The interpretive perspective points to the dangers of excessive reliance on market incentives for innovation, and especially of reproducing the incentive structures of the marketplace in the public arena. But it also highlights certain strengths in American society that have generally been ignored in the broader debate about the country's competitiveness. Three characteristics especially help to position the United States at the intersection of conversational communities that are critical for innovation. One is the standing of our university system in the international scholarly community; the second is the role of immigration, the ethnic and racial diversity of the American work force, and the ethos and ideology of diversity that we have developed in an attempt to accommodate this heterogeneity; and the third is the place of American media in the global culture.

These three features of our society have the cumulative effect of making it easier for us to enter the worlds of foreign consumers while simultaneously reducing the need to do so. The openness of American institutions of higher education and their attractiveness to foreign students and faculty put us at the center of global conversations in virtually every academic field. The effect is to make ours the language of new technologies. People from elsewhere are obliged to enter our world and learn our language, and those of us who grow up in the United States are relieved of the obligation to learn theirs. At the same time, the ethos of American institutions leads them to recruit and incorporate leading scholars from around the world—and to learn the language of foreign scholarship when that scholarship has proved technologically superior to our own.

Our immigrant labor force, to take another example, is essentially made up of interpreters who understand the difference between our world and those of the markets abroad that we seek to enter. Their presence facilitates the redesign of products originally conceived for American consumers so that they fit into the lives of consumers abroad. At the same time, the revolving door of immigration—the fact that so many immigrants return to their home country at least to visit and often to live, bringing with them the objects and understandings of our consumer culture—means that foreigners who never leave their home communities are led to understand the context and meaning of our designed objects.

The preeminence of American movies, television shows, and magazines in the global marketplace operates to similar effect, reducing the distance we have to travel in order to make our products "comprehensible" abroad. American designers do not have to travel to Italy to watch the way people shop or to look at what they are wearing in the street, and how they are wearing it, if Italians pick up American styles by watching U.S. movies.

Finally, in the attempt to manage the growing heterogeneity of American society, we have developed an ideology of diversity, which should make it easier to have the kind of conversations across social and economic boundaries that lead to new interpretive communities. This has not always been the case. Indeed, it has emerged out of public policies developed over the last thirty years in response first to the black civil rights movement and similar social demands for equality among women, people with disabilities, gays and lesbians, and, following the revival of foreign immigration after 1966, a whole variety of new ethnic groups. The effects of this openness to diversity upon the interpretive capacities of the country have yet to be fully felt.

What To Do?

Although the interpretive perspective suggests that American society has hidden strengths that will invigorate the national economy, the fact remains that the basic lessons learned from the expansion of the 1990s give short shrift to interpretation, and the thrust of public policy has been generally hostile to it. Much work remains to be done to strengthen the interpretive capacity of the American economy. How can this be accomplished?

The most direct way to address these problems is to heighten the awareness of managers that interpretation is a process separate from analysis and crucial for innovation. The most striking finding of our case studies is that most managers have at best only a vague awareness of this distinction and a weak vocabulary for thinking and talking about it. A major goal of this book is to give them the vocabulary and conceptual apparatus they seem to lack.

The changes we would like to see in the mindset of American managers cannot be achieved overnight. A place to start is in professional education at engineering and management schools. It is not that interpretation is totally missing from the existing curriculum, especially the management curriculum. The problem is rather that the two perspectives are not clearly distinguished, and the weight given to the analytical perspective is overwhelming. The student is left with the impression that the different kinds of material can be absorbed together—additively, as it were. The independent importance of interpretation and the way it conflicts with analysis are lost. These tendencies in the curriculum and the classroom are reinforced by the scholarly literature. The change we recommend is that the professional schools actively stress the differences between the two approaches, highlight the conflicts between them, and discuss how those conflicts can be managed.

Parallel changes in undergraduate and secondary education are also necessary if we want to nurture innovation in our economy—changes that run against the grain of current reforms at these levels. For example, the drive to strengthen analytical capabilities and computational proficiency in mathematics and science, while it has great merit, lacks balance. It has not been matched by an effort to give students the skills that come through literary critique, historical perspective, language learning, and artistic accomplishment—the kinds of humanistic, holistic studies that broaden and deepen interpretive capabilities.

The second problem is the tremendous pressure on school systems to implement standardized testing in secondary and primary education. Such tests place a premium on questions that are easily evaluated and that lend themselves to quantitative indices of performance. Almost by definition, these tests are antithetical to the cultivation of a tolerance for ambiguity. They do not teach the skills required to generate and live with alternative interpretations. Along with standardized objective tests, therefore, broader essay questions should be required that actively engage students in the interpretive process. Testing of this kind, precisely because it is less objective, cannot be graded easily by machine and hence will inevitably be more expensive than testing analytical skills.

Our point here is not that the emphasis on mathematics and science is misplaced; nor are we arguing against objective, standardized tests. The problem is that lower-level education in the United States has been poor not just in science and math but across the board. We believe that it is necessary to strengthen the quality of the entire curriculum, and that the heavy emphasis on math and science in part reflects a mistaken belief that interpretive skills are unimportant for economic performance.

Rebalancing analytical and interpretive perspectives in the educational system is an essential long-term task. It must be augmented by institutional changes that broaden rather than narrow interpretive spaces in the economy. Public spaces that sustain creativity and nourish innovation over long periods do not grow up naturally in market economies. They need to be created—and once created, they need to be cultivated, enriched, and renewed. And all this must be accomplished while preserving the system of market signals and incentives required for clean, effective, and efficient analytical thinking and decision-making.

Our greatest concern is with the universities. Enticements emanating from the commercial sector and budgetary pressures within the academic community itself are threatening to make the universities increasingly an extension of particular businesses, through special relationships and strategic alliances. The problem we see is not that businesses are being drawn closer to the universities or that particular scholars are drawing closer to business. It is rather that the borders between the two types of institutions have become too porous, putting the university at risk of losing its distinctiveness as a conversational space. This creates three kinds of dangers: first, the danger that the public character of the universities will be compromised; second, the danger that conversation within the universities will replicate conversation in the private sector rather than complementing and enriching it; and third, the danger that within the university itself the research process will becomes less open, more proprietary, and more exclusionary. Increased business involvement in university research can and should enliven the conversation, but that will happen only so long as others who would participate in that discussion are not excluded.

There is a widespread presumption that exclusion is a necessary counterpart of increased business involvement with universities. In our case studies, that view was undermined by firms such as Chiron and Martelli, and even Intel, whose business strategy was to place themselves at the intersection of *inclusive* conversations. As academics ourselves, we are most concerned that research, and especially the research findings around which university conversations take place, remain in the public domain, because the openness of debate about research and scholarship is so central to the academic ethos. But proprietary knowledge also inhibits discussion more generally, and its continued spread will cripple the universities' ability to engage in interpretive conversation with industry. At the very moment when interpretive spaces within the commercial sector are succumbing to pressure from global competition, the academic community may find itself unable to step in and revive the conversation.

Within the university itself, the main threat to inclusive conversation is the disciplinary structure. With their distinctive intellectual dynamics and career rewards, disciplines ensure that the conversations in the universities will never completely duplicate those in the business sector. But university departments are silos in their own right, and they need to be supplemented by interdisciplinary projects, laboratories, and institutes. The case for interdisciplinary interchange is of course not new, but it has become more important as public spaces in the private sector attenuate.

A second crucial domain of public space is the regulatory arena, as we have seen. Regulation has been a focus of intense discussion and debate in the United States over the last three decades, but interpretive aspects of the process have been almost totally neglected. The conversational spaces growing out of the regulatory process in our cases were completely accidental and fortuitous. Partly for this very reason, the regulatory arena may be a promising site for expanding public space, even as conversation in the private sector narrows.

To take advantage of this opportunity, our national perspective on regulation, which has been almost exclusively analytical, will need to widen to include interpretation. The most natural place to do this is in the political process through which regulations are evaluated and revised. Indeed, one can argue that politics itself is an interpretive process. Political debate involves a continual reevaluation of the complex values at stake in society and their relationships to each other in light of the ongoing effort to realize those values in practice. More specifically, in the regulation of particular industries, societal values are evaluated against the technologies that the industry uses. The cost of regulating those technologies—usually experienced as losses in efficiency—is continually compared with the anticipated gains. In our particular cases, those gains took the form of lower health risks in the medical devices sector and more effective communication in the cellular telephone industry. This process of moving back and forth between values and technology, between goals and resources, parallels the way ends and means are continually reinterpreted in the process of product development.

But political debate about regulations poses three problems that will need to be addressed to make it more effective as an interpretive space. First, the debate about the values takes place at too high a level. It occurs through the back and forth between the legislative and executive branches and between those branches and the public at large in congressional hearings, public relations campaigns, and the like. But at this level the debate is too fitful, too episodic, to allow a distinct language community to develop. Such debates are also too far removed from engineers and scientists. These experts are the custodians of the technical relationships under discussion, and yet they are rarely participants in whatever community of understanding about values and constraints eventually emerges. Thus, one need is to develop a deliberative community that is both broader and more continuous than is typically the case.

Second, just as it is difficult to combine analysis and interpretation within a commercial venture, it may be impossible to combine into a single process the deliberative and administrative functions of regulation. Finally, any attempt to use the regulatory process as an interpretive community must address the problem of cooptation, that is, the problem of regulators being drawn into and accepting the perspective of private interests.

A possible model for addressing these issues is the Congressional Office of Technology Assessment (OTA), which for twenty-three years provided advice to Congress on complex science and technology issues before it was closed in 1995 as a cost-cutting measure. With a small professional staff and an extensive network of technical experts and stakeholders drawn from industry, academia, government agencies, and nongovernmental groups of various kinds, OTA responded to requests from congressional committees and its own bipartisan board of senators and representatives for analysis and guidance on often-controversial issues involving the use of science and technology. OTA's domain was not limited to regulatory issues, but its organizational structure and procedures suggest a model for an interpretive space where continuing, technically informed regulatory conversations could occur, separate from the administration of the regulations themselves.[6]

Finally, we need to take a hard look at the state of the intellectual commons.[7] The recent and systematic expansion of private proprietary rights to knowledge—a trend sanctioned by law and enabled by new digital technologies—has been carried out in the name of creativity and innovation. The strengthening of protections afforded to patent holders, the expanded definition of what is patentable, the extension of the duration and scope of copyright protection—all of this has been justified on the grounds of increasing private incentives to invest in creative activities. Whether it is actually producing the desired effect has yet to be established. But even if it is, we see reason for concern.

A consequence of redrawing the boundary between the private and the public in the knowledge domain is to constrain the opportunities for interpretive conversation across organizational boundaries—a fundamental source of our society's creativity. The effect is to restrict who can participate in such conversations and to limit the directions in which the conversations can evolve. A sensible policy for innovation must balance the much-emphasized need to protect private rights to control access to knowledge with the under-appreciated but critical need to protect the public spaces from which economically significant new knowledge so often emerges.

The Creative Economy

We tend to think of economic progress as being driven by the uniquely human capacity for rational analysis. But an equally important component of economic progress is creativity, and creativity is a social process. The mechanism through which it occurs is our capacity for speech, for language, for conversation. That capacity too is uniquely human. The two capacities are fundamentally different—and in that difference, profoundly in conflict.

But we humans are also differentiated by a third capacity—the ability to engage in these contradictory and antagonistic activities simultaneously. What we are not endowed with, however, is the capacity to achieve a balance between them regularly and automatically. Pressures in the environment and in the culture push us in one direction or another. Those pressures vary from society to society; and within each society they change over time. We are living through a period when competitive pressures, emanating from globalization and technological change, have been driving productive organizations toward an increasing emphasis on rational analysis. This trend is reinforced by ideologies that are cultivated in our educational institutions, the media, and the political process. Under the weight of these pressures, the social processes underlying creativity are in danger of being overwhelmed by rational analysis.

Whether the competitive pressures are desirable is an open question. But that is not the question here. In fact, we believe that in our economy there is no serious alternative to accommodating them. Where the debate about America's economic competitiveness has gone wrong, we believe, is in allowing our preoccupation with these pressures—and at times our fascination with and celebration of them—to cloud our collective vision of what is necessary to sustain the innovative performance of the economy. As competition crowds out interpretive spaces in the business sector, we should be securing and expanding those spaces in other kinds of institutions where there is more scope for them. But instead, we are allowing those spaces to be encroached on too, by trying to extend market forces and incentives from the business sector to other parts of our society where they are not inevitable.

Productive societies, to sustain themselves, must be both efficient and creative. The two attributes do not coexist comfortably. The balance between them must in fact be continually reassessed and recreated, especially in periods of rapid economic change. We hope that with this book we have succeeded in providing a useful framework for carrying out this vital task.

NOTES   ACKNOWLEDGMENTS   INDEX

NOTES

1. INTEGRATION IN CELL PHONES, BLUE JEANS, AND MEDICAL DEVICES

1. Welch's advocacy of the "boundaryless organization" was described in a popular management book of the early 1990s by Noel Tichy and Stratford Sherman, *Control Your Destiny or Someone Else Will: Lessons in Mastering Change—The Principles Jack Welch Is Using to Revolutionize General Electric* (New York: Doubleday, 1993). See also Jack Welch and John A. Byrne, *Jack: Straight from the Gut* (New York: Warner Books, 2001).

2. The following description of a cellular system was adapted from Richard K. Lester, *The Productive Edge: How U.S. Industries Are Pointing the Way to a New Era of Economic Growth* (New York: Norton, 1998).

2. WHERE DO PROBLEMS COME FROM?

1. See, for example, Gerald Pahl and Wolfgang Beitz, *Engineering Design: A Systematic Approach* (New York and London: Springer, 1996); David G. Ullman, *The Mechanical Design Process* (New York: McGraw-Hill, 1992); W. S. Lovejoy, "Rationalizing the Design Process," presented at the Conference on Design Manage-

ment, Anderson Graduate School of Management, University of California at Los Angeles, September 17–18, 1992; John Hauser and Don Clausing, "The House of Quality," *Harvard Business Review*, May–June 1988, pp. 63-73; Karl T. Ulrich and Steven D. Eppinger, *Product Design and Development*, 2nd ed. (New York: McGraw-Hill/Irwin, 1999).

2. Herbert A. Simon, *The Sciences of the Artificial*, 2nd ed. (Cambridge: MIT Press, 1981).

3. Nam P. Suh, *The Principles of Design* (Oxford: Oxford University Press, 1990).

4. K. B. Clark and T. Fujimoto, *Product Development Performance: Strategy, Organization, and Management in the World Auto Industry* (Boston: Harvard Business School Press, 1991).

5. Frederick P. Brooks, *The Mythical Man-Month: Essays on Software Engineering*, anniversary ed. (Boston: Addison Wesley, 1995).

3. CONVERSATION, INTERPRETATION, AND AMBIGUITY

1. Paul R. Carlile, "A Pragmatic View of Knowledge and Boundaries: Boundary Objects in New Product Development," *Organization Science* 13, no. 4 (July–August 2002): 442–455.

2. In developing our understanding of interpretation and communication, we have drawn on an extensive scholarly literature. Three strands of that literature have been particularly influential: language studies, hermeneutics, and Heideggerian philosophy. This literature and its relevance to our argument is summarized in Michael J. Piore, Richard K. Lester, Fred M. Kofman, and Kamal M. Malek, "The Organization of Product Development," *Industrial and Corporate Change*, 3, no. 2 (1994): 405–434. We have drawn especially on Hubert L. Dreyfus, *Being-in-the-World: A Commentary on Heidegger's Being and Time, Division 1* (Cambridge: MIT Press, 1991); George Lakoff, *Women, Fire and Dangerous Things: What Categories Reveal about the Mind* (Chicago: University of Chicago Press, 1987); and Terry Winograd and Fernando Flores, *Understanding Computers and Cognition: A New Foundation for Design* (Reading, MA: Addison-Wesley, 1987). For a more extensive review of this literature, see Kamal Malek, "Analytical and Interpretive Practices in Design and New Product Development:

Evidence from the Automobile Industry," unpub. Ph.D. thesis, Department of Mechanical Engineering, MIT, 2001.

3. Lakoff, *Women, Fire and Dangerous Things*.

4. Annabelle Gawer, "The Organization of Platform Leadership: An Empirical Investigation of Intel's Management Processes Aimed at Fostering Complementary Innovation by Third Parties," unpub. Ph.D. thesis, Sloan School of Management, MIT, 2000.

5. Clayton M. Christensen, *The Innovator's Dilemma* (Boston: Harvard Business School Press, 1997).

6. Ibid., p. 134.

4. THE MISSED CONNECTIONS OF MODERN MANAGEMENT

1. John Hauser and Don Clausing, "The House of Quality," *Harvard Business Review*, May–June 1988, pp. 63–73.

2. Katie Hafner, "From Phone to Fashion, Nokia Style," *New York Times*, December 9, 1999, Section G, p. 1.

3. Kamal Malek, "Analytical and Interpretive Practices in Design and New Product Development: Evidence from the Automobile Industry," unpub. Ph.D. thesis, Department of Mechanical Engineering, MIT, June 2001.

4. Ronald S. Burt, *Structural Holes: The Social Structure of Competition,* Cambridge: Harvard University Press, 1992.

5. Douglas North, *Institutions, Institutional Change and Economic Performance* (New York: Cambridge University Press, 1990).

6. Michael Polanyi, *The Tacit Dimension* (Gloucester: Peter Smith, 1983).

7. See Daniel Barbiero, "Tacit Knowledge," in C. Eliasmith, ed., *Dictionary of Philosophy of Mind*, http://www.artsci.wustl.edu/~philos/MindDict/index.html. Also, Arthur Reber, *Implicit Learning and Tacit Knowledge: An Essay on the Cognitive Unconscious* (New York: Oxford University Press, 1995); G. Ryle, *The Concept of Mind,* rpt. ed. (Chicago: University of Chicago Press, 1984).

8. Alfred Marshall, *Principles of Economics* (New York: Macmillan, 1920), pp. 267–277. F. Pyke, G. Becattini, and W. Sengenberger, eds., *Industrial Districts and Inter-firm Cooperation in Italy* (Geneva: International Institute for Labor Studies, 1990). Annalee Saxenian, *Regional Advantage: Culture and Competition in Silicon*

Valley and Route 128 (Cambridge: Harvard University Press, 1996).

9. Donald A. Schön, *The Reflective Practitioner: How Professionals Think in Action* (New York: Basic Books, 1990).

10. Ikujiro Nonaka and Hirotaka Takeuchi, *The Knowledge-Creating Company: How Japanese Companies Create the Dynamics of Innovation* (New York: Oxford University Press, 1995).

11. Paul R. Lawrence and Jay W. Lorsch, *Organization and Environment: Managing Differentiation and Integration* (Boston: Graduate School of Business Administration, Harvard University, 1967).

12. Ronald S. Burt, *Structural Holes: The Social Structure of Competition* (Cambridge: Harvard University Press, 1992).

13. Lawrence and Lorsch, *Organization and Environment.*

14. Peter Senge, *The Fifth Discipline: The Art and Practice of the Learning Organization* (New York: Currency Books, Random House, 1990).

15. Karl E. Weick, *Sensemaking in Organizations* (New York: Russell Sage Publications, 1995); Karl E. Weick, *Making Sense of the Organization* (Oxford: Blackwell Publishers, 2000).

16. "Organizational Redesign as Improvisation," in Karl E. Weick, *Making Sense of the Organization*, pp. 57–91.

17. Jan Michl, "Form Follows WHAT? The Modernist Notion of Function," *Magazine of the Faculty of Architecture and Town Planning*, Technion, Israel Institute of Technology, Haifa, Israel, 10 (Winter 1995): 31–20 [sic].

18. "Bauhaus: History\Ideologies\Achievements\Typography," at http://people.ucsc.edu/~gflores/bauhaus/b1.html.

5. COMBINING ANALYSIS AND INTERPRETATION

1. The particle-wave analogy is particularly apt, we think, in the sense that waves are like interpretation, continuous, whereas the discrete acts into which analysis divides behavior are like particles.

2. See Annabelle Gawer, "The Organization of Platform Leadership: An Empirical Investigation of Intel's Management Processes Aimed at Fostering Complementary Innovation by Third Parties," unpub. Ph.D. thesis, Sloan School of Management, 2000; also, Annabelle Gawer and Michael Cusumano, *Platform Leadership:*

How Intel, Microsoft, and Cisco Drive Industry Innovation (Boston: Harvard Business School Press, 2002).

3. Ten years after the original Cardinal project was abolished, the company revived the idea in an attempt to stimulate new product development.

4. Both the Bell Labs and Cardinal examples raise the question as to whether the company really should try to create within itself two radically different organizations with diametrically opposed approaches to business. They suggest that at least a rudimentary appreciation of the need for both approaches is required *throughout the organization* if one is not eventually to eclipse the other.

6. PUBLIC SPACE

1. See Alfred Chandler, *The Visible Hand: The Managerial Revolution in American Business* (Cambridge: Harvard University Press, 1977); Robert Solow, "The New Industrial State or Son of Affluence," *Public Interest,* no. 9 (Fall 1967); John Kenneth Galbraith, "Reply," *Public Interest,* no. 9 (Fall 1967).

2. Douglas K. Smith and Robert Alexander, *Fumbling the Future: How Xerox Invented Then Ignored the First Personal Computer* (New York: William Morrow, 1988).

3. Alfred Marshall, *Principles of Economics,* 9th ed. (London: Macmillan for the Royal Economic Society, 1961).

4. See, for example, Martin Kenney, ed., *Understanding Silicon Valley: The Anatomy of an Entrepreneurial Region* (Stanford, CA: Stanford University Press, 2000); F. Pyke, G. Becattin, and W. Sengenberger, eds., *Industrial Districts and Inter-firm Cooperation in Italy* (Geneva: International Institute for Labor Studies, 1992), esp. G. Becattini, "The Marshallian Industrial District as a Socioeconomic Notion," pp. 37–51.

5. Falvia Farinelli, "Networks of Firms Confronting the Challenge of Globalization: Italian Case," Institute for Prospective Technological Studies, European Commission Joint Research Center Report Issue 07, September 1996.

6. J. A. Cantwell and S. Iammarino, "MNCs, Technological Innovation, and Regional Systems in the EU: Some Evidence from the Italian Case," Discussion Papers in International Investment and

Management, Reading, UK, 1998; M. Storper and B. Harrison, "Flexibility, Hierarchy and Regional Development: The Changing Structure of Industrial Production Systems and Their Forms of Governance in the 1990s," *Research Policy*, 20, no. 5 (October 1991): 407–422; Hubert Schmitz, "Small Shoemakers and Fordist Giants: Tales of a Supercluster," *World Development*, 23, no. 1 (January 1995): 9–28.

7. Busco Sabastiano, "Small Firms and the Provision of Real Services," paper presented at the International Conference on Industrial Districts and Local Economic Development, Institute for Labor Studies, International Labor Organization, Geneva, 1990.

8. Steven Weber, *The Success of Open Source* (Cambridge: Harvard University Press, 2004).

9. Rohit Sakhuja, "Air Interface Standards for Digital Mobile Cellular Systems in the U.S., Europe, and Japan," unpub. M.Eng. thesis, Department of Electrical Engineering and Computer Science, MIT, 1995.

10. Steven Epstein, *Impure Science: AIDS Activism and the Politics of Knowledge* (Berkeley: University of California Press, 1996).

11. Michael Lipsky, *Street Level Bureaucracy: Dilemmas of the Individual in Public Services* (New York: Russell Sage Foundation, 1983).

12. James Q. Wilson, *Varieties of Police Behavior: The Management of Law and Order in Eight Communities* (Cambridge: Harvard University Press, 1968).

13. Charles F. Sabel, "Design, Deliberation, and Democracy: On the New Pragmatism of Firms and Public Institutions," in K.-H. Ladeur, ed., *Liberal Institutions, Economic Constitutional Rights, and the Role of Organizations* (Baden-Baden: Nomos Verlagsgesellschaft, 1997), pp. 101–149.

14. See Archon Fung and Dara O'Rourke, "Reinventing Environmental Regulation from the Grassroots Up: Explaining and Expanding the Success of the Toxics Release Inventory," *Environmental Management*, 25, no. 2 (February 2000): 115–127; Archon Fung, Dara O'Rourke, and Charles Sabel, *Can We Put an End to Sweatshops?* (Boston: Beacon Press, 2001); Archon Fung, "Accountable Autonomy: Toward Empowered Deliberation in Chicago Schools and Policing," *Politics and Society*, 29, no. 1 (March 2001).

15. See Gabriel Kolko, *The Triumph of Conservatism: A Reinterpreta-*

tion of American History, 1900–1916 (New York: Free Press, 1963); George Stigler, "The Theory of Economic Regulation," *Bell Journal of Economics and Management Science,* 2, no. 1 (Spring 1971): 3–21; Richard Posner, "Theories of Economic Regulation," *Bell Journal of Economics and Management Science,* 5, no. 2 (Autumn 1974): 335–358.

16. Pamela Campos, "Organizational Integration in Situations of Uncertainty: A Case Study of MITRE Corporation," unpub. S.M. thesis, Technology and Policy Program, MIT, 1999.

7. UNIVERSITIES AS PUBLIC SPACES

1. In addition to the case studies, our discussion of this topic also draws on several other sources, including a faculty seminar at the Industrial Performance Center on the evolution of the research university and a series of theses on the same subject prepared by our students. See Sachi Hatakenaka, *University-Industry Partnerships in M.I.T., Cambridge, and Tokyo: Storytelling across Boundaries,* Studies in Higher Education Dissertation Series (London: Routledge, 2003); Jean-Jacques Degroof, "Spinning Off New Ventures from Research Institutions outside High-Tech Entrepreneurial Areas," unpub. Ph.D. thesis, Sloan School of Management, MIT, 2002; Carlos Martinez-Vela, "The Challenge of Integration in the Research University," unpub. S.M. thesis, Technology and Policy Program, MIT, 1998; Sean Safford, "Why the Garden Club Couldn't Save Youngstown: Social Capital and the Transformation of the Rust Belt," unpub. Ph.D. thesis, Sloan School of Management, 2004.

2. About 60 percent of the funding for academic research provided by industry is for basic research. In 2000, industry spent $1.4 billion on basic research at universities, up from $705 million in 1990, but still much less than the $14.2 billion of industry-financed basic research carried out in industry itself. See National Science Board, *Science and Technology Indicators—2002,* Appendix Tables 4-3 and 4-7.

3. Edward B. Roberts, "Global Benchmarking of the Strategic Management of Technology," Industrial Performance Center Working Paper MIT IPC 99-007WP, MIT, December 1999.

4. One such initiative was the Bayh-Dole Act of 1980, intended to promote university patenting and licensing to industry. Other prominent initiatives include the National Science Foundation's Science and Technology Centers and Engineering Research Centers, both of which make government research funding for universities contingent on industry participation.

5. A thoughtful assessment of the promise and limitations of technology-mediated distance education is presented in John Seely Brown and Paul Duguid, *The Social Life of Information* (Boston: Harvard Business School Press, 2000), esp. chap. 8.

6. Over the past decade a group of academic economists has made a series of important contributions to this subject. See, for example, N. Rosenberg and R. R. Nelson, "American Universities and Technical Advance in Industry," *Research Policy*, 23, no. 3 (1994): 323–348; E. Mansfield, "Academic Research and Industrial Innovation," *Research Policy*, 20 (1991): 1–12; R. Henderson, A. B. Jaffe, and M. Trajtenberg, "Universities as a Source of Commercial Technology: A Detailed Analysis of University Patenting, 1965–88," *Review of Economics and Statistics*, 80, no. 1 (1998): 119–127; D. C. Mowery, B. N. Samprat, and A. A. Ziedonis, "Learning to Patent: Institutional Experience, Learning, and the Characteristics of U.S. University Patents after the Bayh-Dole Act, 1981–1992," *Management Science*, 48, no. 1 (2002): 73–89; W. M. Cohen, R. Florida, L. Randazzese, and J. Walsh, "Industry and the Academy: Uneasy Partners in the Cause of Technological Advance," in R. Noll, ed., *Challenges to Research Universities* (Washington, DC: Brookings Institution Press, 1998).

7. Rosalind Williams, *Retooling: A Historian Confronts Technological Change* (Cambridge: MIT Press, 2002). See also Seely Brown and Duguid, *The Social Life of Information*, for a similar view.

8. The dual analytical–interpretive nature of university research was also highlighted recently by MIT professor Eric Lander, who had just been appointed as the director of a major new genome research laboratory affiliated with MIT and Harvard. At an MIT faculty meeting, he described the two kinds of activities that the new laboratory would undertake: scientific "programs" and scientific "platforms." "Programs," Lander explained, are communities bringing together groups with common interests to share ideas,

identify needs and opportunities, and collaborate in the organization and operation of research. "Platforms," by contrast, are professionally run organizations that are able to carry out complex projects which might require the development of a new technology or the use of a cutting-edge technology. Lander's vocabulary was different from ours, but the two activities clearly correspond to the interpretive–analytical duality.

9. Michael D. Santoro and Alok K. Chakrabarti, "Corporate Strategic Objectives for Establishing Relationships with University Research Centers," *IEEE Transactions on Engineering Management*, 48, no. 2 (May 2001).

10. See W. M. Cohen, R. R. Nelson, and J. P. Walsh, "Links and Impacts: The Influence of Public Research on Industrial R&D," *Management Science*, 48, no. 1 (2002): 1–23.

11. Donald E. Stokes, *Pasteur's Quadrant: Basic Science and Technological Innovation* (Washington, DC: Brookings Institution, 1997).

12. One of the most recent instances at MIT is the Computational and Systems Biology Initiative, which brings together ideas and concepts from the biological sciences, engineering disciplines, and computer science.

13. For example, nearly 41 percent of engineering graduate students and 39 percent of graduate students in mathematics and computer sciences in the United States are foreign citizens. At the faculty level, 33 percent of senior engineering faculty and 40 percent of senior computer science faculty are foreign born. See National Science Board, *Science and Engineering Indicators— 2002*, Appendix Tables 2-20 and 2-27.

14. MIT Industrial Performance Center Faculty Seminar, "The Entrepreneurial, Global University," March 14, 2000.

15. James D. Watson, *The Double Helix: A Personal Account of the Discovery of the Structure of DNA,* rpt. ed. (New York: Charles Scribner, 1998).

8. LEARNING THE RIGHT LESSONS ABOUT COMPETITIVENESS

1. Testimony of Bruce P. Mehlman, assistant secretary of technology policy, U.S. Department of Commerce, before the House of Rep-

resentatives Committee on Small Business, June 18, 2003, at http://www.technology.gov/Testimony/BPM_030618.htm.

2. Lawrence Lessig, *The Future of Ideas: The Fate of the Commons in a Connected World* (New York: Random House, 2001).

3. For a practical discussion, see Alistair Cockburn, *Surviving Object-Oriented Projects* (Reading, MA: Addison-Wesley, 1998).

4. Frederick P. Brooks, *The Mythical Man-Month: Essays on Software Engineering,* anniversary ed. (Reading, MA: Addison-Wesley, 1995). See also Peter McBreen, *Software Craftmanship: The New Imperative* (Reading, MA: Addison-Wesley, 2002).

5. Alexandro Artola, "Implications of Nearshore Development in the Mexican Software Industry," unpub. M.Eng. thesis, Department of Electrical Engineering and Computer Science, MIT, 2003. See also Kyle Eischen, "Working through Outsourcing: Software Practice, Industry Organization, and Industry Evolution in India," Center for Global, International, and Regional Studies, University of California at Santa Cruz, Working Paper 2004-04, 2004.

6. For a historical perspective on OTA, see the notes and electronic publications archive contained in "The OTA Legacy" at http://www.wws.princeton.edu/~ota/.

7. See also Lessig, *The Future of Ideas.*

ACKNOWLEDGEMENTS

A very large number of people have contributed, directly and indirectly, to this book. First and foremost are the managers and engineers in the companies we visited. They not only provided the raw material from which our arguments emerged, but many of them also entered directly into the intellectual endeavor, sometimes helping us to formulate new ideas and sometimes persuading us to discard old ones.

Over the years we have benefited from conversations with many colleagues who were generous with their insights, suggestions, and time, including Tom Allen, Alex D'Arbeloff, Douglas Dayton, Michael Dertouzos, John Ehrenfeld, Olivier Favereau, Woody Flowers, Bob Gibbons, Gary Herrigel, Patrick le Quément, Frank Levy, Rick Locke, Tom Malone, Joel Moses, Ed Roberts, Chuck Sabel, Warren Seering, Bob Solow, Peter Temin, Karl Ulrich, Jim Utterback, and Harry West. Early in our research we met several times with Don Schön, who, among many other valuable contributions, staged a design simulation game for us. Readers will hear echoes of Don's voice throughout this book.

Our research partner in the formative years of the project was Fred Kofman, then a faculty member of the Sloan School. Fred was our co-author on an early article laying out the intellectual agenda for the research. Kamal Malek was a participant in much of the field work while doing his own doctoral research at the IPC; in the great MIT tradition, he went on to form a company to develop some of the ideas in his dissertation. We are also grateful to our students Alexander Artola, Dan Breznitz, Pam Campos, Sachi Hatakenaka, Carlos Martinez-Vela, Sean Safford, and Rohit Sakhuja for their helpful observations and criticisms. Many other colleagues and students, too numerous to mention by name, have participated in related activities at the IPC over the past several years, notably including the Center's Globalization Project, Local Innovation Systems Project, and two stimulating faculty seminars, one on the future of the research university and the other on the role of narrative in the social sciences.

We owe special thanks to our friend and colleague Suzanne Berger, who throughout this project has been a constant source of encouragement, incisive critique, and constructive suggestions. Joan Magretta read an early draft of the manuscript, pinpointed its weaknesses, and helped launch us in a different direction. We also thank Hervé Dumez, Tony Friscia, and Joseph Onek for their careful readings of the manuscript at critical moments in its development.

Our research could not have been carried out without the long-term financial support provided to the Industrial Performance Center by the Alfred P. Sloan Foundation. Several of the Foundation's officers also participated in our discussions and made substantive contributions as the project unfolded. We are particularly grateful to Hirsh Cohen, Ralph Gomory, and Gail Pesyna. Additional financial assistance was provided by Coopers & Lybrand, as it then was, and the MITRE Corporation. Both Coopers and MITRE also gave us access to their own projects and personnel for small case studies that supplemented the principal cases on which the book is based.

Acknowledgements

At Harvard University Press, we especially thank Michael Aronson for supporting, shepherding, and championing the book, and Susan Wallace Boehmer, our smart, sympathetic, and demanding editor.

John Arditi and Deborah Garrity provided staff support and editorial assistance for the multiple working papers and articles that preceded the final manuscript. And above all we are indebted to the IPC's administrator, Anita Kafka, whose enthusiasm, cheerful efficiency, and ingenuity in finding countless ways to help move the project forward represent the best in MIT's administrative tradition.

INDEX

computer industry *(continued)*
59, 60, 113; hardware products,
113, 181; chip development and
production, 130, 181; compatible products, 132; networks,
178; economic development
and, 181; offshore operations,
183–184; software development,
183–184. *See also* Personal computers

consultants, 75, 135, 144–145, 152

conversations, 94, 105; direction
of, 8, 11; difficulty with, 10–11,
96; role of manager in, 11, 49,
52; interpretive process and, 12,
53, 57, 121, 129, 147; new product design and, 47, 56, 67–68,
70, 72, 76–78, 80, 175; across
boundaries, 49, 185, 192; *vs.*
problem solving, 49–50; ambiguity in, 51, 55, 56, 57, 62–63,
112; new product development
and, 51, 62, 78; vocabulary, 51;
organizational barriers to, 52;
focus on objects and practices,
52–53; open-ended, 53, 63, 68–
69, 75, 102, 135, 159, 175, 179;
misunderstandings and ambiguity in, 53–54, 57, 60, 62–63, 69–
70, 73, 122, 176; as communication, 55; interpretive, 55, 56, 69,
160, 161, 174–175, 176, 178; climate of suspicion and mistrust,
60, 121, 135; disclosure of competitive assets in, 60, 121; exchange of information during,
61; new topics for, 64, 175; with
customers, 67–68, 97, 100; in
language communities, 73;
about core competencies, 85;
momentum of, 95, 175; about
regulation, 105, 130, 132–133,

141, 190; organizational restructuring and, 109; communities
for, 112, 118; as collaborations,
113–114; breakdown of com
munication in, 119, 121–122;
competition and, 119, 121; secrecy and suspicion in, 119, 121,
176; R&D, 124; sheltered spaces
for, 125, 126; governance structures and, 126; direct (face-to-
face), 130, 134, 180; internal,
143–144; at research universities, 160–161; withdrawal from,
166–167, 176; language developed in, 167; public, 170–171;
interpretive management and,
175; in the private sector, 177,
189; global, 184–185;
cooptation, 142; FDA and, 144

copyright protection, 192

core competencies, 4, 5, 84–88; focus on, 11, 76, 88; analytic view
of, 85; competition and, 85; conversations about, 85; integration
of new product development
and, 85; interpretation and, 85;
networks and teams, 85–86; in
cellular telephone industry, 86–
88

corporations: focus, 4, 5; mission
statements, 4; transformations
in, 4; virtual, 75; conglomerates,
84; integrated, 84; as bureaucracies, 89; lifecycles, 108–110; organizational restructuring at,
108–110; as public space, 122,
123–125; sheltered spaces
within, 123–124; internal conversations, 143–144; funding for
research universities, 149; in-
house R&D, 149; external
sources of technology, 150; re-

Ericsson, 17, 30; switching technology, 86, 87; core competencies, 88; marketing strategy, 102; management problems, 103; organizational restructuring at, 103, 104; specialization at, 103; organizational structure, 103–104; compatibility of products with other producers, 133

Federal Aviation Administration (FAA), 142
Federal Communication Commission (FCC): regulation at, 129–134, 136
Federally Funded Research and Development Centers (FFRDCs), 142
Fifth Discipline, The (Senge), 92
flexibility, 75; in manufacturing, 78; in management, 89; lack of, 172
focus groups, 27, 52
Food and Drug Administration (FDA), 144–145; regulation at, 134–138; cooptation and, 144
Ford Motor Company, 84
France Telecom, 17
Fujimoto, Takahiro, 45

Gap, The, 46
garment industry, 18, 79, 85; boundary management in, 32–33; heavyweight manager in , 46; style in, 46; design teams, 46–47; test stores and retail outlets, 119–120; Italy, 125; New York, 125; Paris, 125; design operations, 152, 182–183; market, 153
globalization, 2–3, 9, 124, 180, 193; competition and, 174, 189

GSM digital standard, 30–31, 102–103

hearing aids, 28, 109
heavyweight managers, 45–46, 47; *vs.* conversation, 58
hermeneutics, 198n2
Hewlett-Packard: medical imaging market and, 23, 64–65; alliance with Philips Medical Systems, 23, 64–65; engineering teams, 48; internal structure and boundaries, 48; technological concept at, 65; business units, 67; software products, 128
hip-hop music, 81, 82

IBM, 125, 181; software products, 128
immigration, 184, 185, 186
improvisation, 93
industrial districts as public spaces, 122, 125–129
Industrial Performance Center, 203n1
information: technology (IT), 2, 75, 78, 143, 173, 180, 181; uncertainty, 93; leakage, 115, 119; exchange, 117; appropriation of, 176; flow, 179. *See also* Intellectual property; Knowledge
innovation, 96, 153, 154, 170, 175, 188; growth in the 1990s, 4, 5; in the economy, 4–5, 171, 173, 176, 177; as determinant of future prosperity, 5; economic policy and, 5; interpretation and, 6, 8–10, 9, 10, 177; in new products, 8, 173; in case studies, 10; commercial viability of, 25; market-driven, 25–26, 58, 170; problem solving and, 42; analytical man-

agement of, 43; organization of, 43; systematization of, 43–44; disruptive, 65–69; conditions for, 70; language and, 70; premature disclosure of, 121; performance and, 171; United States' position in, 171; conversational communities for, 184; market incentives for, 184; policy for, 192

Innovator's Dilemma, The (Christensen), 65–68

integration, 172; organizational issues surrounding, 10, 14, 45, 75; through additions of departments and divisions, 10; across boundaries, 14, 23, 33; among departments or divisions, 14; between company and outside partners, 14, 25–26; between producers and consumer, 14, 23, 27–28; during design and production, 23–27; boundary management in, 29; specialization and, 91, 104; by systems people, 104; coordination and, 184

Intel, 59–60, 112–113, 181; competition, 113–114; interactions with smaller firms, 113–114, 126; strategic development at, 113–114; conversational space at, 118–119; chip development at, 130; microprocessor production, 130; business strategy, 189

intellectual property, 127, 163, 178

Internal Revenue Service (IRS), 142

International Organization for Standardization (ISO), 43

Internet, 4, 41, 108, 126; new business spawned from, 178–179

interpretation/interpretive perspective, 6, 63, 67; innovation and, 6, 8–10, 177; management and, 8, 9, 11, 65; *vs.* analysis, 10, 11–12, 34, 53, 54–55, 65, 69, 92, 93, 94, 97–98, 107; sheltered spaces for, 12; differences with analysis, 34, 200n1; ambiguity and, 53, 112, 133; in conversations, 53, 55, 56, 57, 121, 147; as open-ended process, 53, 175; product development and, 54, 121, 143; creation of interpretive space, 71, 72; of customer's voice, 83; core competencies and, 85; vocabulary for, 89, 117; communities of, 91, 94; understanding of, 93; ongoing nature of, 97, 139, 200n1; product lifecycle and, 100–108; public space and, 119, 120, 153–163; *vs.* analysis, 122, 123, 153, 174, 186–187, 200n1; regulation and, 130, 136, 141, 146; maintenance and management of, 137–138; bureaucratic rules and, 140; benchmarking and, 140–141; at research universities, 154–155, 166, 169; creativity in the economy and, 170; public policy and, 186; scholarly literature on, 198n2

ISO 9000, 43–44

Italy, 126; Levi Strauss and Co. trips to, 28, 47, 48; industrial districts, 90; blue jeans and garment industry, 114–115, 116, 125

iteration: problem solving through, 37, 38; in new product design process, 77; as analytical strategy, 97

regulation *(continued)*
    merging horizons and, 140–145;
    as interpretive process, 141; de-
    sign of, 142; ambiguity in, 146;
    criticism of, 146; role in market,
    146; of technology, 190; inter-
    pretive-analytic framework for,
    190–191; administration of reg-
    ulations, 191, 192. *See also* De-
    regulation
"regulatory capture" concept, 142
Renault, 81
Replay, 114
research: communities, 22; medi-
    cal, 22; at academic laboratories,
    23; new product development,
    36–37, 60; centralized labs, 124;
    within corporations (internal),
    144; social interactions and, 154;
    motivation for, 157–159, 165;
    financial gains from, 158, 166,
    168; fundamental character of,
    158; conversations in, 159, 160–
    161; problem solving in, 159; in-
    terdisciplinary, 160; interpretive
    conversations for, 161; secrecy
    surrounding, 164–165, 166;
    funding for, 168, 203n2; indus-
    trial liaison programs, 168; as
    shared knowledge, 168; industry,
    168–169; proprietary, 169; basic,
    178, 203n2; government, 178;
    costs of, 203n2. *See also* R&D
research universities, 12, 148–153,
    184; disciplinary structure of,
    149, 159, 163–165, 167, 189–
    190; collaboration with industry,
    149–150; commercialization of,
    149–153; market and, 150; pro-
    prietary curricula, 150; aca-
    demic structure of, 151; eco-
    nomic role of, 151–153; as

public space, 153, 161, 167; cur-
    ricula, 154, 159; analytical and
    interpretive dimensions of, 154–
    155, 161, 162; collaboration at,
    155, 178; problem selection at,
    155–156; practical motivation
    at, 156; interpretive activity at,
    156–157, 159–160, 162, 163,
    166, 169; participants, 159–160;
    conversations at, 160–161, 162,
    164, 166, 188–189; competition
    within, 162–163, 166; interpre-
    tive-analytic framework for, 163;
    boundaries in, 164, 165–169; se-
    crecy surrounding, 164–165;
    ethos of openness at, 166, 167,
    168, 184; industry involvement
    in, 167, 168; conflict of interest
    at, 168; embedded corporate
    laboratories at, 168; proprietary
    arrangements at, 168; halfway
    houses for industry collabora-
    tion, 168–169; flow of informa-
    tion at, 179; foreign students
    and faculty, 184–185, 205n13;
    corporate involvement in, 188–
    189; proprietary knowledge at,
    189; silos within, 190; patent-
    ing and licensing to industry,
    203n4
retail outlets, 28, 46, 79, 119–120
rules: formal, 90, 133, 138; infor-
    mal, 90; application of, 139; bu-
    reaucratic, 140

sales forces: interaction with new
    product developers, 31–32; cli-
    nicians and doctors as salespeo-
    ple, 58, 135
Senge, Peter, 92
"sense-making," 92–93
sequential design process, 131–132